Christ at the Door

Christ at the Door

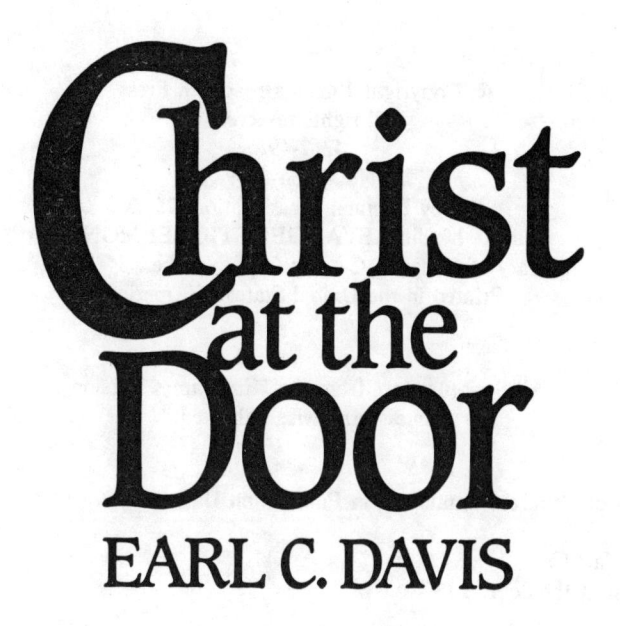

EARL C. DAVIS

BROADMAN PRESS
Nashville, Tennessee

© Copyright 1985 • Broadman Press
All rights reserved
4262-49
ISBN: 0-8054-6249-X
Dewey Decimal Classification: 252.3
Subject heading: EVANGELISTIC SERMONS
Library of Congress Catalog Card Number: 84-27441
Printed in the United States of America

All Scriptures are from the King James Version,
unless otherwise indicated.

Library of Congress Cataloging in Publication Data

Davis, Earl C.
　Christ at the door.

　1. Evangelistic sermons.　2. Baptists—Sermons.
3. Sermons, American.　I. Title.
BV3797.D27C49　1985　　　252′.06132　　　84-27441
ISBN 0-8054-6249-X

Dedication

To my son Deryl who, when he was but four years old, asked me three of the most profound questions in the world: "Daddy, does God love us?" "Daddy, why does God love us?" and a last question, "Daddy, do we love God?" by which I knew Christ was knocking at his door

Contents

1. The Triple Tragedy 9
2. The Convenient Season... 21
3. The Reality of Hell 29
4. Born to Be a King 39
5. A Salvation We Can Understand............................ 50
6. What Is Special About Christianity? 61
7. Coats and Christianity 69
8. The Daring Young Man.. 78
9. The Diary of a Lonely Woman 87
10. Pretonius... 95
11. Why Is the Devil So Mad?....................................106
12. Abraham: No Easy Faith 116
13. Ships and Havens..128
14. Christ at the Door 139
15. One Life, One Death, One Account....................149
16. A Stairway to God 161
17. What Goes Up Doesn't Have to Come Down 173
18. Heaven's Gates and the Gypsies...........................182
19. The Heartbreak of Backsliding 190
20. The Gospel of the Second Chance 200
21. The King Is Coming: Closing Time......................211

1
The Triple Tragedy
Luke 15

I will arise and go to my father, and will say unto him, Father, I have sinned against heaven, and before thee (Luke 15:18).

It has been called the greatest short story in the world. Truly, when other books crumble into dust and the world has waxed old like a garment, this story will still be young and fresh. And yet this remarkable story, which we call the parable of the prodigal son, is but one of three connected stories the Master told which Luke has recorded in the fifteenth chapter of his Gospel: the tragedies of the lost sheep, the lost coin, and the lost boy.

For you and me to feel the heart of these stories, we must try to recreate the scene when Jesus first told them to people just like us.

These parables were told when opposition to Jesus had hardened. He is on His way to His cross and the chosen people have rejected their calling—"He came unto his own, and his own received him not." Picture a day like that one when a paralyzed man was let down through the roof to be healed by Jesus. When He healed the man by the word of forgiveness, the scribes and Pharisees began to gripe and grumble about His comments on forgiveness, completely overlooking the fact that the man was healed. Or the day when Levi, a notorious sinner and tax collector, walked away from his old life to follow the master, and threw a grand feast to celebrate—and Jesus came, of course! The scribes and Pharisees? They merely muttered and complained that a religious teacher would stoop to eating with such a sinner!

The Tragedy of the Cold Ones

And so the first of the three tragedies of our text has to do with the attitude of the religious folks toward God's wonderful work of grace. In verses 1 through 3 we see the tragedy of the cold people of God: And the Pharisees and scribes murmured, saying, This man receiveth sinners, and eateth with them. And he spake this parable unto them, saying, . . ."

The climax to the three stories, the shadow behind them, is the portrait of the elder brother in the prodigal son parable. He is clearly a picture of how Jesus feels about church people who claim they know God and want to be like Him, and yet turn away from the poor and the outcast, the misfits who would come from the darkness of sin into the circle of fellowship and love of the church if we would only welcome them! No church can have revival if it is filled with "elder brothers"—and sisters!

I don't like to dwell on this first tragedy, but we must for a moment more, until we each come to grips with how repulsive this attitude is to Jesus. There is a huge hypocrisy in our churches as we proclaim in our newspapers, radio, and TV ads—not to mention the church yard sign—that "*everybody* is welcome," yet too often we really do not want those folks who are not exactly like us.

How well I remember the fiery old deacon who always wanted to hear more of the blood, yet was an elder brother. A family of sharecroppers had moved in on the main road just outside the little village where I pastored. My wife and I had been picking up the kids for Sunday School and church for several Sundays, although it was considerably off our beaten path. Now, since this deacon passed by that house on his way in to church, it seemed right to ask him to pick the family up. The first Sunday things went fine—but the second Sunday when I asked him to bring the family, he balked. Surprised, I questioned him, and his honest answer was, "They smell bad, and I don't want them smelling up my car." My, how we elder brothers say we want the dirty, ragged, different sinners to come to Jesus—but just don't ask *us* to welcome them to the Father's house!

Look further at the mirror of the elder brother in verse 28, which takes place when the ragged prodigal comes and the rejoicing begins. The elder brother hears the merrymaking while still in the field and calls a servant to explain. Upon hearing the "good" news "he was angry, and would not go in: therefore came his father out, and entreated him." Can you see it? He "boiled over" with anger at taking the prodigal back. His thoughts are on himself: "I never transgressed . . . you never gave me . . . but when *this* one . . . !" See him sulking in the hot afternoon out behind the house!

What an unattractive character the elder brother is! I would hate to be cooped up with him all day in a bass boat, or have to spend the morning with him in a duck blind or under the same tree at a dove shoot! He may well be the reason the prodigal left home! He makes the committed Christian rethink the list of most serious sins: the repentant prodigal was welcomed with a kiss by the father, who most surely represents God in this eternal portrait, while the scribes and Pharisees, who are just as clearly the elder brother, are definitely a disappointment to God.

The Tragedy of the Lost Ones

The second of the three tragedies of this beautiful chapter is that of our lost condition. There is a haunting emphasis in all three parables on *lostness*. There is the lost sheep, first of all. And here I think we are justified in hearing the Master talk of a certain kind of lostness. The sheep of the story became lost through its own curiosity, wandering away, following its own foolish notion, with no thought to its danger. Never bothering itself with cautions, never looking up to get its bearings, merely munching its way on to confusion, danger, and destruction.

One of the grand old saints in my church was seeking to combat this kind of "wandering-off lostness" which is a result of our inherent bent toward sin, when he counseled his teenage grandson. Said the saint, "You ought to stay in the habit of going to church regularly, Son. If you don't, you will run with the nonchurch-going and non-Christian bunch. And if you do that, you will probably marry a girl who is not a Christian and does not go to church. If you do that, you will completely drop out of church. If you do that, your children will grow up pagans!"

That's putting it bluntly and honestly. And that kind of wandering which leads to lostness is almost second nature to us all. It is especially fostered in our culture which puts the emphasis on "doing your thing," which leads to troubled and frustrated youth falling prey to all kinds of cults, drug pushers, and the pull of materialism.

And as in the grandfather's fears, so often the wandering lostness leads to the second kind of lostness: that of the coin. The situation of the coin is different from that of the sheep, yet just as deadly. Through no fault of its own, the cherished coin, no doubt part of the cherished symbolism of the married state worn by Jewish women much as we wear our wedding rings—rolled away. And I can see, in the images our Master used here, the pitiful condition of little children who, because of circumstance, parental neglect, environment, or lack of concern by Christians, roll off as human coins and fall unnoticed into the dark corners of life. And we cannot ignore the words of Jesus: "It were better [for that man who makes the children to stumble] that a millstone were hanged about his neck, and that he were drowned in the depth of the sea" (Matt. 18:6). There is a tremendous spiritual responsibility which parents and churches have toward children.

The third picture of lostness is of yet another kind—that of the deliberately rebellious boy. One of the best descriptions of the this young man is given by James Weldon Johnson:

> The Younger son said to his father,
> Father, Divide up the property now and give me
> my portion,
> And the father, with tears in his eyes, said:
> "Son, don't leave!"
> But the boy was stubborn in his head,
> And haughty in his heart,
> And he took his share of his father's goods

And went into a far country.

There comes a time,
There comes a time
When every young man looks out
From his father's house,
And longs for that far-off country.

The young man journeyed on his way,
And he said to himself as he traveled along,
This sure is an easy road,
Nothing like the rough furrow
Behind my father's plow.

Young man,
Young man,
Smooth and easy is the road that leads to hell—
Down-grade all the way . . .
No need to trudge, and sweat, and toil,
Just slip and slide, slip and slide
Til you bang up against hell's iron gates![1]

This boy deliberately went lost; home was tedious to him; it fretted and chafed him; he wanted his "freedom." And so Jesus portrays in this parable the illusion of liberty without responsibility.

Jesus saw every soul as lost—like the sheep through thoughtlessness; like the coin through common participation in the web of sin which surrounds us all; like the boy who embraced a deliberate rebellion against his father.

And Jesus saw the inevitable course of sin in our lives and projected it into the sad conclusion of the prodigal son's adventure: an inner disintegration, outer misery, and total ruin. Such is the message of the picture, so abhorrent to the Jew, of the boy sitting by the pig trough.

The Tragedy of the Searching One

The third of the triple tragedies of Luke 15 is that of the sorrowful and searching Father. Yet I must point out that while it is truly the tragedy of the sorrowing Father so long as we turn from His love and care, within this picture of the Father there is a striking emphasis on the persistent, patiently-searching Father.

God is as concerned for His children as any man ever was for a lost lamb; as concerned as any new bride ever was over the loss of the marriage headband coin. Elizabeth Clephane wrote these touching words:

> Lord, Thou hast here Thy ninety and nine,
> Are they not enough for Thee?
> But the Shepherd made answer: "This of Mine
> Has wandered away from Me,
> And altho the road be rough and steep,
> I go to the desert to find my sheep.

> But none of the ransomed ever knew
> How deep were the waters crossed;
> Nor how dark was the night that the Lord passed thro'
> Ere He found His sheep that was lost.
> Out in the desert He heard its cry—
> Sick and helpless, and ready to die.

The Pharisees never dreamed of God searching for man! Yet it is clear as we listen to Jesus telling these stories that we have *misnamed* them all! It is not the story of the *lost sheep*—but rather of the *good shepherd*. It is not the story of the *lost coin*—but rather of the *searching wife*. It is not the story of the *lost boy*—but rather of the *loving father*. And in each case, the emphasis is on the joy of finding that which is lost:

> But all thro' the mountains, thunder-riv'n,
> And up from the rocky steep,
> There arose a glad cry to the gate of heav'n,
> "Rejoice! I have found My sheep!"
> And the angels echoed around the throne,
> "Rejoice, for the Lord brings back His own!"

The Pharisees had given up on those who most needed help, those caught most tightly in the web of sin. But as an unknown preacher once observed: "He who thought most seriously of the disease called it curable; those who thought less seriously called it incurable." And perhaps the greatest compliment of Jesus to man—certainly the most hopeful word—is in the phrase describing the prodigal boy: "And when he came to himself. . . ." Although the boy first came to grief, he then came to himself, and finally to his father.

Let us add to the lost condition of every person, and the everlasting picture of the searching God, the possibility of repentance—going home again, in every life. And the boy comes home, rehearsing all the way how he will confess and ask his father to let him be like the hired hands. And the boy came home, back up the road, in repentance, down which he had ridden away in pride and rebellion.

And the father sees him coming, limping up the path. At first the father shades his eyes with his hand and studies the ragged figure and then, heart pounding, tears running down his rugged face, and beard flying in the breeze, he runs down the lane to hug his prodigal—home at last!

I can see the faces in the crowd around Jesus as He told

these stories. Some are drawn and bitter from a life of hardness and alienation from God and man; some are etched with the ache of rejection; some are painfully innocent; some have tears feeling their way down cheeks unnoticed. For some, hope, like a dove, lights in their hearts as the Master speaks of "coming home."

As we quietly let the Holy Spirit apply the Master's story to our hearts, listen now to a touching modern story of one who "came home." The story is from Ian Maclaren's *Beside The Bonnie Brier Bush* and is set in Scotland. It begins on that day when Lachlan Campbell, a pillar of the kirk, stood up and in sepulchral tones asked the assembly to strike the name of his only daughter from their roll. As he unfolded the story through tears to the minister, and showed him with trembling hands the letter from his daughter, it was all so clear.

Lachlan's wife, Flora's mother, had died when Flora was a babe. Flora was the joy of her father's life, but, now, as a young woman, she had made her decision to disappear and seek excitement and happiness in the big city.

The news of her leaving spread, and one afternoon Marget Howe, one of those saints God gives every community, came to comfort Lachlan. Her son, George, had died years earlier while studying for the ministry, and now her words ran something like this: "I had a son, and he is gone; you had a daughter, and she is gone . . . I know where George is, and I am satisfied. I think your sorrow must be deeper than mine. . . ." To which Lachlan replied, "Would to God she were lying in the kirkyard, too!" He then took the family Bible and showed Marget how he had blotted out Flora's name in great wavering strokes, but the ink was blurred as if it had been mixed with tears.

Marget went away and wrote to Flora a letter of the heart, one part of which went like this: "I am writing this tae say that yir father luves ye mair than ever, and is wearing oot his hert for the sicht o'yir face. . . . The glen is bright and bonny noo, for the purple heather is on the hills, and doon below the gowden corn, wi'bluebell and poppy flowers between. Naebody 'll ask ye where ye've been, or onything else . . . yir father bids ye come, and I'm writing this in place o'yir mother."

Marget showed her letter to Lachlan before mailing it, and he walked with her to the crest of the hill en route to the post office and watched her become a tiny speck on the road. Then he went back to his cottage, and in the twilight and lengthening shadows he realized: "It iss in the dark that Flora will be coming, and she must know that her father iss waiting for her." He cleaned and trimmed the lamp carefully and set it in the window, on the large family Bible in which he had blotted out her name, for a stand. And every night until Flora came home its glow shone down the path, like the love flows down from the open door of our Father's house.

Flora came home soon after . . . sick in body and soul, but home again in her father's house. And lying there on her sickbed, she told her father how she came home.

"It was a beautiful night in London, but I will be thinking that there is no living person caring whether I die or live. . . . Crowds passing, but no one to whom the name Flora meant anything, and not one sore heart if I died that night." She crept into the shadow of a church and wept. And then the noises of the street passed away, "and I was walking to the kirk with my father—and I saw my home, and the flowers that I had planted, and the lamb coming for her milk, and I heard myself singing. . . ." And there was singing, for the church was open, the light was streaming out the open door, and they were singing the old hymn—"There is a fountain filled with blood."

She went in and sat down at the door. The sermon was on the prodigal son, "but there is only one word I remember—'you are not forgotten or cast off,' the preacher said: 'You are missed,' and then he will come back to it again, and it was always 'missed, missed, missed.' Sometimes he will say, 'If you had a plant, and you had taken great care of it, and it was stolen, would you not miss it?' and I will be thinking of my geraniums, and saying 'yes' in my heart. And then he will go on, 'If a shepherd was counting his sheep and there was one short, does he not go out to the hill and seek for it?' and I will see my father coming back with that lamb that has lost its mother. My heart was melting within me, but he will still be pleading, 'If a father had a child, and she left her home and lost herself in the wicked city, she will still be remembered in the old house, and her chair will be there,' and I will be seeing my father all alone with the Bible before him . . . and there is no Flora."

She slipped out of the church and went to her room, wondering if even God cared, and hoping for a sign. There she found the letter from Marget, and its promise: "Your father loves you more than ever." Soon she was on the train, and all night she journeyed, coming home.

As she finished her story, her father rose and got the family Bible, and opening it to the family register where his daughter's name had been blotted out, he bowed his head:

"Will you ever be able to forgive your father?" Flora took the pen and wrote in the Bible for a moment, and when her father lifted his head, this is what he read:

Flora Campbell
Missed April 1873
Found September 1873

"Her Father fell on her neck and kissed her."[2]
"I will arise and go to my father."

2
A Convenient Season
Acts 24:24-27

And he said unto another, Follow me. But he said, Lord, suffer me first to go and bury my father. Jesus said unto him, Let the dead bury their dead: but go thou and preach the kingdom of God (Luke 9:59-60).

One of the chief sins of mankind is procrastination—the deadly sin of putting things off. In fact, I've been putting off this sermon too long. I am not alone in my sin of procrastination—it strikes us all; preachers, barroom gamblers, tiny children, beautiful ladies, gray-headed patriarchs, and politicians.

Our attics are full of projects we may never get around to doing anything with. Our desks are cluttered with memos we keep shuffling from folder to folder. Our minds are filled with the ghosts of resolutions made year after year in January and just as regularly broken and forgotten in February. Our hearts are filled with good intentions that so often fall by the wayside from neglect.

Our text story is a tragic example of the deadly sin of procrastination in the spiritual realm. Antonius Felix was the procurator of Judea from AD 52 to 60. His name "Felix" means "happy," but it is doubtful if this man ever knew what true happiness was.

Paul was arrested in Jerusalem following his third journey, you will recall, and after the threat of riots, the Roman tribune Claudius Lysias wrote a letter to Felix in Caesarea and sent Paul to him.

Paul was followed to Caesarea by the high priest Ananias and the Jewish elders, who "informed the governor against Paul." All this served to arouse Felix's curiosity, so he commanded a centurion to keep Paul, allow him liberty, and detain none of his friends from visiting Paul.

A few days later Felix brought his Jewish wife Drusilla, one of three wives Felix had in his career, to talk with Paul. The Scripture tells us they

> heard him concerning the faith in Christ. And as he reasoned of righteousness, temperance, and judgment to come, Felix trembled and answered, Go thy way for this time; when I have a convenient season, I will call for thee (Acts 24:24-27).

That "convenient season," the season in which Felix would listen to the gospel and give serious consideration to the abundant life in Christ, never came. As far as we know, his procrastination robbed this man of his salvation and eternal life!

Procrastination: The Jeopardy of Souls

Jesus rebuked in strong terms the spirit of procrastination, of putting off. Luke records the response of a man whom Jesus called to follow him: "Lord, suffer me first to go and bury my father. Jesus said unto him, Let the dead bury their dead: but go thou and preach the kingdom of God."

In Luke 14 Jesus enumerates in the parable of the great supper the excuses given by the guests when the time for the feast arrives. One needs to look over a piece of land he has just purchased—as if a man would buy land without first examining it! Another has just acquired five yoke of oxen, and needs to go look at their teeth! The third has an excuse more difficult to fault—he has just gotten married! The master of the house and host of the feast is angry, and commands others to be invited, saying: "none of those men which were bidden shall taste of my supper" (v. 24).

Now Jesus' view is quite clear: "Seek ye *first* the kingdom of God and his righteousness." (Matt. 6:33, author's italics). Get the priorities straight and march ahead without hesitation or delay.

The Convenient Season Which Never Comes for Church Folks

To procrastinate in worldly matters may cost the student a scholarship; the salesman a valuable contract or promotion; the tycoon a fortune; the soldier a victory. But to procrastinate in spiritual matters puts in jeopardy a person's eternal soul.

Seldom does a Christian intend to go through one's entire life giving God the peelings, the stray dollar, the lip service. Yet many Christians in every church are doing exactly that—giving God the hulls of their lives by putting off the spiritual disciplines necessary to walk truly with God.

We so often lament our ignorance of the Bible, yet the daily newspaper receives much more attention from most church members than the Bible. We protest we are hungry for God's Word, yet a large proportion of every church's membership skips the hour of Bible study.

Some say the church is cold, a little clique runs everything. Sound familiar? Yet these same critical folks are never at church on Sunday evenings or Wednesday evenings, and are never willing to invest their time and energy into the work of the church!

I am right on target when I declare that procrastination has robbed more church members of the joy of their salvation than all the dark sins combined. Jesus condemned this attitude of putting off, waiting until later, because it is a fundamental sign of our rebellion against God. When we drag our feet in the Lord's work, it writes volumes about our kinship to Adam!

And a tragic footnote to the procrastination of the Christian concerning joyful service of the Lord is that this attitude is seen by the nonbeliever. *If the church member feels that way, and has those values,* reasons the nonbeliever, *why should I be in a hurry to be so miserable?*

The Convenient Season Which Never Comes for the Lost

Somewhere I heard of a conference Satan held on the enticement of sinners. He posed this question to all the devils and imps in attendance: "What is the best way to keep a person from confessing Jesus Christ as Lord and Savior?" One young imp proposed: "Tell them there is no God!" There were murmurs of approval all around the table. But Satan said there was a better approach.

After some brainstorming, another imp suggested, "Whisper to them that there is a God, but he doesn't care about the souls of men!" Amid chuckles of glee Satan demanded yet a better approach. In a fit of bedeviled inspiration the idea was put forward: "Have them believe that there is a God, that He loves them—but that He is helpless to save sinful men!" There was general merriment and a roar of applause. But Satan sat grim-faced and finally shared his secret; the most successful way to prevent a sinner from coming to Jesus: "Don't hinder him from hearing that there is a God; that God loves the sinner and even sent Jesus to die for his sins: *just keep whispering in the sinner's ear that he need be in no hurry; he has plenty of time to come to Christ!*"

I don't think a single person has ever told me they just did not plan ever to become a Christian. What folks say is that they plan to start to church *sometime;* they plan to respond to the gospel invitation *sometime;* they plan to join the church *sometime*—just not right now. Later, when they are settled in the new house, when they get the car fixed, when they get the baby ready to stay in church, whatever.

The Inconvenient Season Which Always Comes

There is an inconvenient season that is sure to come in every person's life more than once. A time when it "were worth worlds to know Jesus Christ as Savior." Indeed, when it is a strength beyond the world's knowing to have Him as the Lord of death, the Comforter of the afflicted, and to know that He has been where we are in that dark night of the soul.

Felix, who bade Paul wait until "a convenient season" to share the glories of faith in Jesus Christ, experienced the inconvenient season. A few years after talking with Paul, Felix's son perished in the catastrophic eruption of Mt. Vesuvius. Like many another parent, all he could do was wail "My son, my son."

There drops the dark veil of the inconvenient season

when we ourselves face death. I will never forget a white-headed old man I met during a revival effort twenty years ago. Helping a fellow seminary student to "run a meeting," we were out making evangelistic visits. As we drove up, chickens scattering and the old hound dog skulking closer under the porch, I saw him—suspenders, chair propped back against the wall, squinting at us in the glaring sun.

Our efforts to share Jesus with him were met with courtesy, but his final summary revealed that he was waiting for the convenient season which, in my judgment, might never come. Said he, "twixt the stirrup and the ground; mercy sought and mercy found." Now, I was dumbfounded to hear this bit of poetry, and have mused upon it these twenty years. Apparently taken from a description of warfare in other days, it describes how the fatally wounded horseman seeks and finds mercy as he is shot out of his saddle. What a tragic approach—to gamble on being able to bargain with God in your last moment of life! What a terrible misunderstanding of what the new life in Christ is all about! I have often wondered if that old man ever made a genuine commitment of his life to Jesus.

We cannot say to the coffin, burnished in the lamplight, "Go thy way—I will call for thee in a more convenient season!" Nor to the anguish of a midnight phone call, "Come again some more convenient season!" Nor can we command the disease that wasteth at noonday—"Be gone! Come again some more convenient season!"

Twin Truths of Every Season

The Bible teaches twin truths that stand firm in every season: (1) Life is uncertain, and (2) it is as great a tragedy to have lived a long, empty life as to have your life cut off short. Life is uncertain, and we should not tarry in making certain of the welfare of our immortal souls.

Every gardener knows what is responsible for the failure of most gardens. Not the lack of rain, not the scorching sun, but mere neglect. Neglect will allow the weeds to take over and gradually choke out and destroy the vegetables. And that is all you have to do to destroy your immortal soul—just neglect it. Just put off the pleading of the Holy Spirit, the urging of your friends.

Somewhere I read of the sad death of Thomas Carlyle's wife. It seems she was confined to bed for months with a lingering illness. Her gifted husband worked downstairs at his writings. Sometimes in the afternoons he would go up to her bedroom and spend time with her, but not nearly enough.

Then came the dreary day when the heartbroken husband trudged through the rain behind a coffin bearing his wife. After the funeral he came back to the empty house in despair, and went upstairs to weep.

Seeing her diary lying on the bedside table, he took it up and began to read random entries. On a page would be a notation like this: "He spent an hour with me today, and it was like heaven. . . ." On another page: "I wonder if he will come this afternoon. . . ." And on one page: "It's getting dark; I don't guess he's coming today." And all the remorse of his soul could not change what might have been, what should have been. He had let the convenient season pass by, and now in the inconvenient season he had no strength.

The idea of someone waiting for each of us is a deep and moving image. In the parable of the prodigal son, Jesus draws the picture of the father who is waiting for the son to come home. Many of our old gospel songs speak of the waiting father, and our coming home.

Do not tarry this day, putting off the decision for Jesus which you want to make, need to make, and ought to make. This is the most convenient season you will ever have.

I never preach on procrastination without thinking of the story of the scientist who went to the Southwest to make a study of a particular species of bird. It was hard to find, and even harder to observe and study. He watched some of these birds flying up into a cave under a ledge in a canyon wall. So off he hiked to do his studies in the canyon. Tying a sturdy rope to the top of the canyon wall, he lowered himself down to the ledge and then below it, kicking off the wall and swinging back under the ledge into the cave. Once there, he untied his rope and set a rock on top of its end to keep it from being pulled out of the cave and beyond his reach. He had just turned away and pulled out his lamp when he heard a noise. Looking around, he saw the rope's end swinging out over the canyon, having come loose. He quickly assessed his situation: He *must* catch the rope on the first swing of its "pendulum"—it would be closer than ever again. If he failed, he would be trapped in the cave.

It may be the kingdom of God is swinging closer for you right now than it ever will again. Will you seize it?

3
The Reality of Hell
Luke 16:19-31

For I have five brethren; that he may testify unto them, lest they also come to this place of torment (Luke 16:28).

Are Icebergs for Real?

It was the graven image of the age. Twice as long as St. Paul's Cathedral in London, if you could stand it on end, it would have reached within 100 feet of the top of the Eiffel Tower.

Its decks were the fantasy of some decorator, with trellises and trailing ivy. There was a gymnasium and a swimming pool. Every stateroom had a telephone. It was a millionaire's ship—loaded with every creature comfort one could have imagined in those lavish years just after the turn of the twentieth century. The only lack was lifeboats; there were only half enough for the number of crew and passengers.

I said it was a rich man's fantasy, and the passenger list read like a society list for the world. There was John Jacob Astor on his honeymoon, Ben Guggenheim of that fortune, Major Archibald Butt, aide to President Taft, and many more of the wealthy and famous. It was said that the combined wealth of the passengers on the ship that night was over two-hundred fifty million dollars in 1912 monetary terms!

Maybe that was one reason she sailed on in the face of common sense. After all, what iceberg would dare get in the way of such a distinquished crowd? Maybe that is why nobody worried about the lack of lifeboats—what could happen to such a company of the world's "in" people.

And even though the murky fog of the North Sea quickly settled in on the behemoth, surely no passenger standing at the rail staring into the unknown had apprehensions—for, after all, this ship was unsinkable. She was double-hulled and even divided into sixteen watertight compartments if the unthinkable happened.

And so the pride of the White Star Line, the ultimate in luxury, sailed from Southampton, England, on April 10, 1912. Bound for New York on this maiden voyage were 1,400 passengers and 940 crew, plus a copy of Edward Fitzgerald's translation of *Omar Khayyam* in a binding containing 1,500 precious stones, each set in gold.

Uppermost in the captain's mind was speed. The coveted Blue Riband for the fastest crossing of the Atlantic had been in German hands since 1897, and both crew and passengers knew this was more than a mere crossing. The pride of England was at stake. To capture, on her maiden voyage, this glorious title would make complete the honor of this unsinkable queen of the seas.

That year the North Atlantic ice packs broke up early and began to menace shipping far sooner than usual. As the *Titanic* steamed west, other ships began to radio warnings of wandering icebergs. One ship, *The Californian,* finally gave up about 11 PM on April 11 and stopped its engines to wait for daylight before picking its way through the "minefield" of the North Atlantic.

It is interesting that *The Californian* twice tried to warn this unsinkable queen of the sea, the last time about 7 in the evening, and was cut off before the message was completed. After all, the wealthy had messages they needed to radio to America.

True, the captain did double the lookouts. But since nobody thought to provide the men in the crow's nest with binoculars, it did little good. Apparently, it was more important to make sure that the fresh water supply did not freeze in the rapidly-falling temperature.

It happened at twenty minutes before midnight. Most passengers didn't even notice it. A slight jolt, a jar—nothing dramatic to indicate that the mightiest ship on the sea, the *Titanic,* had received a mortal wound. But the ship had struck an iceberg, and it had slit her "unsinkable" hull as you slit a baked potato—leaving a gash 300 feet long. Seawater cascaded into the terrible wound, flooding five of the sixteen watertight compartments. The captain sent for the ship's carpenter, but he was already dead below.

It was a pathetic scene, with the captain pleading with the people to "be British." Colonel Astor helped his bride into a lifeboat, told her he would see her in New York, then leaned over the rail and lit a cigarette. Ben Guggenheim sent a message to his wife: "If anything happens to me, tell my wife I have done my best in doing my duty." Then both he and his valet put on evening clothes for the sinking.

Ten miles away the crew of *The Californian* slept. Only the officer of the watch noticed the rockets from the dying ship, and he thought it was merely a fireworks display! Two hours and forty minutes later, the unsinkable *Titanic* slipped beneath the cold waves, taking with her over 1,500 souls!

First reports of the tragedy to reach New York were chaotic. One account stated the passengers were in no danger, while a later release affirmed that the watertight compartments were holding well; some reports had the *Titanic* under tow by another ship, and when it was finally admitted she had sunk, the report stressed that no lives were lost!

Ignoring the reality of something we dread even to contemplate will not make it go away. You and I marvel at the refusal of *The Titanic*'s masters to take seriously the danger of icebergs. And yet, some of you hearing these words persist in ignoring the reality of hell, as if to ignore it will make hell go away. Such wishful wishing is both pathetic and fatal.

Is Hell for Real?

Why do we ignore hell? I think for many it is because we reject the scare tactics of yesteryear. Also involved is the emphasis on science, and its argument that there is no geographical place out there, or down there, or in there, called hell. Still others feel that the idea of hell is somehow inconsistent with a loving God. Surely, we say, if God loves us all, He will not send anyone to hell.

Jesus Believed in Hell

I want to stress in no uncertain terms that Jesus believed in hell. He believed in an immeasurable danger that threatened the souls of men; He had a horror of a great darkness from which they had to be delivered; He saw a dreary desert of exile toward which men strayed.

Jesus preached judgment and final separation of the good and the evil on the last day. He spoke of the weeds and the good wheat, which may grow together and even be indistinquishable now, but will be divided at the last day. He spoke of the fishermen who, while fishing, keep whatever the net receives, but at the dawn dump all the catch on the beach and divide the good fish from the bad. He spoke of the salt which had lost its flavor and was good for nothing but to be cast on the wayside. He spoke of the door being shut; of people coming from the north and south, east and west to sit down in the kingdom of God with Abraham, Isaac, and Jacob—and you yourself being left out. (see Luke 14:25-30.)

Jesus described hell in terms of the gnashing of teeth, weeping and wailing, outer darkness, the second death, burning fire, and the trash heap, Gehenna. Over two hundred times the New Testament speaks of outer darkness and punishment. It is difficult to read the Bible and not ponder the meaning of the stories Jesus told of Lazarus and the rich man, the sheep and the goats, or the great judgment scene in the Book of Revelation.

Questions About Hell

There are many questions we all have about hell. Some are unanswerable, but we keep on asking them anyhow!

"Will there be degrees of torment?" It would seem so, although we should not be dogmatic about these matters. A reading of the following passages dealing with this area may give some light. Luke 12:47-48, the conclusion of a parable Jesus told about servants, teaches that the servant who deliberately disobeyed his master's will was punished severely, while the ignorant servant was more lightly punished. Romans 2:5-6 is part of Paul's comments that a man may, through his hardness and impentitent heart, store up the wrath of God. It seems that varying degrees of rebellion would bring varying degrees of punishment. Second Corinthians 5:10 declares that we must all appear before the judgment seat of Christ, to receive recompense for the deeds done in the body, and, obviously, even among the lost, sinful deeds do vary.

"Will we know about those who go to hell?" I had a phone call late one night recently, and a distraught lady asked me if it were true that in the Book of Revelation we are taught that after this world is done, God will open up a window of heaven, and we who are in heaven will be given a brief glimpse of those writhing in torment in hell, then the window will be forever closed. I told her it was neither a teaching of the Book of Revelation nor an accurate portrayal of the nature of God!

There is, however, no grounds for a "blotter" theory, no biblical basis that I can see for the idea that our lost friends and loved ones will be forever forgotten, even though we might prefer that as the best possible solution. Surely we will not be more ignorant in heaven than on earth! I rather think that, being more like God, we will be able to handle the sad knowledge that some folks dear to us will not be in heaven. For the meaning behind the idea of Lazarus being "in Abraham's bosom" (v. 22) is that he was having fellowship with him, which would require memory. And Dives recognized Lazarus in the afterlife, and pleaded that he be sent to Dives's brothers, whom he also remembered.

"Maybe we just go to purgatory for a little while and then on to heaven?" No way, biblically. That is wishful thinking. Our everlasting condition is fixed in *this* life, and we apparently cannot be laundered in purgatory. This truth is underscored by the "great gulf" (v. 26) Jesus mentioned in this parable.

"Do unbelievers go immediately to hell when they die?" It is important for us to realize that the Bible is much more clear and plain when it deals with the future of the saved folks than when it speaks of the future of the lost people. The Christian goes immediately to be with the Lord, and the lost go to hell.

There are three main views about the reality of hell and its possible duration. Scripture teaches that hell is everlasting, as is heaven. Some other folks prefer to believe in universal salvation, so that there is no need for a hell of any duration. We all would desire this to be true, but "wishing doesn't make it so!" A third view is that there is no hell, just as there is no heaven. Like the old dog Rover, when we die, we die all over. Both these last two views are wishful thinking, and they can deceive a person into neglecting his eternal salvation.

A Perspective on Hell

Before I briefly summarize the biblical teaching on hell, be sure to let a couple of things sink in. First, always *remember that eschatology*—what will happen in the end—*is a working out of the contradiction between what IS and what OUGHT to be.* What you see and experience in life—the sin, corruption, injustice, and inhumanity to man—is not what God intends, and the scales will be balanced in the end. Secondly, we must understand the reality of hell in the context of *man's rebellion, God's mercy in Jesus,* and *man's rejection of Christ.* Hell is not a plaything of God, dreamed up one afternoon. Such a view better fits schoolboys who catch flies and pull off their wings. Hell was never part of God's plan for men.

The P's of Hell

Hell is a *Prepared Place.* I know this sounds like a contradiction of what I have just said, but I want to stress that hell was *not* prepared for you or me. It was a result of the rebellion of Satan. Jesus tells us in the parable of the sheep and the goats: "Then shall he say also unto them on the left hand, depart from me, ye cursed, into everlasting fire, *prepared for the devil and his angels*" (Matt. 25:41, author's italics). When a person chooses hell, he goes to a place prepared for the devil, not for men. God prepared another place where He yearns for all men to go (see John 14:1-3). But, God has known from eternity how He would discard the devil and those who would come under his dark dominion, and in light of this terrible reality, He sent Jesus.

Hell is a *Permanent Place.* Again, our text seems to stress this aspect of hell. Hell is no halfway house to heaven. In a novel entitled *Diary of a Country Priest,* the priest, tired of both him and his gospel being ignored, finally tells his congregation in words like these: "You have refused to hear me day after day—but one day the Word will be heard of men . . . not the voice you rejected, quietly saying 'I am the Way, the Truth, and the Life,' but a voice from the depths saying 'I am the Door forever locked, the Way that leads nowhere, the everlasting Dark.' "[1] Hell is the door forever locked, the way that leads nowhere, the everlasting dark.

Hell is a *Punishment Place.* But what, you ask, is the

medium of punishment? Some preachers love to ring the changes of hell on the concept of fire, and I do not deny that; but remember fire is the symbol for terrible misery and loss. I think hell is best—or worst—perceived of in terms of *loss* and the reality is worse than the symbol. Loss, first of all, of God. As surely as heaven is best defined as the presence of God, so hell is the absence of God forever.

Let me illustrate what I mean when I say hell is best seen as loss of God's presence. Picture in your mind the most wicked man in your city. Can you see him? Good. Now, this man knows he can call on God and be saved if he truly repents any hour of the day or night. He knows your pastor will get out of bed at midnight, or three in the morning—and do it gladly—to share the love of Christ with him. But, brethren, there is coming a time in the life of the unsaved person when he will not have that opportunity. He will be beyond the reach of the gospel. I can think of nothing worse than that!

Hell is loss of fellowship. Loss of friendship. Somewhere I read the following quote which is right on target about the loneliness of hell: "No more screamingly irrational an idea has ever been foisted onto a gullible public by the father of lies than the view that hell will be a place where the roistering of good fellows will raise the roof with gaiety and cheer!"

Hell is loss, and awareness of it. Apparently, and unfortunately, folks in hell lose everything but memory, personality, and the ability to think and suffer and despair.

Hell Is a *Preferred Place.* Jonathan Edwards, in his celebrated sermon, "Sinners in the Hands of an Angry God," left the impression that God dangles sinners over the pit of hell much like a puppeteer dangles his puppets. Every now and then the flames singe the strings, and a sinner falls into hell. That is not at all the case! God sends no one to hell. Judgment Day will simply reveal the decision you have made during your life about heaven or hell. If you go to hell, you will do so because you have chosen it. God has done everything not only humanly possible, but also divinely possible, to keep you out of hell. Therefore, if you go, you will *choose* to go to a place which was *not prepared for you, and where you were never intended to be.* Jesus said, "Him that cometh to me I will in no wise cast out" (John 6:37).

Now, why preach on hell, anyhow? I never feel good after preaching this sermon. I preach on hell not because of curiosity about the temperature or furniture of hell, but because the important fact of hell is decided *here and now,* in this life. Jesus spoke of hell, not to say you were going there, but to warn you so you might escape!

Some folks are going to hell, but *you* don't have to! Your blessed alternative is to choose the salvation God offers in Jesus Christ. This day, this night, this very hour you can make the decision about where you will spend eternity. And you'll never have to worry about it again! Will you turn from your sins—turn from the road to hell—and invite Jesus into your heart?

4
Born to Be a King
(An Old Testament Narrative Sermon)
2 Samuel 14:25

But in all Israel there was none to be so much praised as Absalom for his beauty: from the sole of his foot even to the crown of his head there was no blemish in him (2 Samuel 14:25).

The Bible is the most powerful book in the world. It has power not only because it holds the key to our overcoming the sin that dogs our hearts, but because it is a mirror of human nature. In the fairy tale of "Snow White and the Seven Dwarfs" the wicked queen had the magic mirror which she consulted when desiring to preen both her countenance and her ego. The only problem was the mirror was honest; ruthlessly so. "Mirror, mirror on the wall; who is the fairest of them all?" And one day the mirror replied that the wicked queen was runner-up to Snow White!

Just so does the Bible honestly tell us about ourselves. To read the accounts of the men and women of the Bible is to look in an old family photo album. To consider their sins and folly is to see wherein we fall short.

So let us look at one story in the Old Testament. It is the story of one particular father and one particular son, yet it is the story of every father and every son, and it is the story of our Heavenly Father and all of us.

It is a story of greatness; great promise, great sin, and great tragedy. It is the story of a boy who was raised in the lap of luxury; he had everything a boy could desire—he was born to be a king! He was born with a silver spoon in his mouth and a scepter in his hand! He even built for himself a monument in the king's dale, and called it by his own name. I never read the story of this young man without thinking of another young man, years ago in one of my pastorates. His father was very wealthy, and a trust fund had already been established for the boy. At the age of twenty-one, he could walk into the bank and write a check for one million dollars! But it ruined him; he knew he would never have to work, never have to prove himself, never have to raise a hand to feed himself. He was already, as a teenager, good for nothing. Such is the danger of being born to the purple. But let us hasten to our story.

Our tale begins in the streets of old Jerusalem, on market day. There are the usual sights of the market—the merchants putting up their bright canopies and setting their wares out to tempt the passersby, the early housewives with baskets on their arms, farmers with their vegetables and livestock. There are the usual smells of the market—the warm smell of baked goods, the pungent smells of perfumes offered by the vendors, the earthy smells of animals, the rich smell of hot sunshine on leather. There are the sounds of market day, too—the shrill voices of housewife and merchant haggling over a cut of lamb or a piece of cloth or a dried fish, the clopping of the hooves of camels and sheep on cobblestones, the fluttering of caged doves, the bleating of sheep, the chatter of gossip.

The Prince Who Stole the People

In the midst of such a scene there comes a whisper like the ripples on the water: "He is coming! Look! Look!" And sure enough, in the center of a crowd he moves through the marketplace, somehow managing to look humble, friendly, and concerned, while all the time protected from the people by the close-knit curtain of an honor guard of handpicked soldiers.

This is the prince, and he is going to the main city gate. There he will mingle with the elders of the city who gather there to hold court, so to speak. For here, just inside the city gate, the gray heads gather to hear disputes, to argue issues, to pass judgments. It is akin to a city court. And here the prince often comes.

To the battered merchant who has been robbed, the prince declares with fervor, "My friend, I don't know why the government doesn't do something about these bands of hoodlums!" To the farmer brought to his knees by the drought, the prince says in sympathetic tones, "My heart aches for you, my brother, and one day we'll have folks in high places who listen to your troubles and do something!" He puts his arm around the shoulder of the old woman in poverty and agrees, "It's a shame that we don't take care of folks like you—if we had the right leaders, this wouldn't be!"

How vividly is this undermining of the king sketched for us in 2 Samuel 15! The indictment of the writer of this record closes with the succinct statement: "So Absalom stole the hearts of the men of Israel" (v. 6). But something is wrong here! This is Absalom, King David's son, who is speaking against the king! Why is he doing that? Why would any son try to undermine his father?

And here the story takes a gigantic leap into the twentieth century and into your life and mine, and into the lives of our sons and daughters. Absalom is a son alienated from his father. He both hates and loves his "old man." He is being ignored and feels that destruction is the best—and perhaps only—way he can be heard. David is a confused father. He is torn about his son. It has been five years since he has spoken to his son or seen his face.

How Did Such a Thing Happen?

The seeds for the scene of Absalom at the gates stealing the hearts of the people goes as far back as the sin of David and Bathsheba, but we will trace it only to a terrible sin of seven years earlier, when another son of David, Amnon, forced his sister Tamar to have sex with him. Absalom's anger at this sin smoldered for two years, during which time David apparently never lifted a finger in judgment. Finally, at a feast during sheepshearing time, Absalom had his brother Amnon killed. Terror spread through the countryside, and Absalom fled the country, not knowing if his life might be forfeited.

Three years the prince lived at Geshur in exile, while his father longed for reconciliation, but took no steps to bring it about. Finally General Joab—brave, foolish Joab—took matters into his own hands. He persuaded a poor woman of Tekoah to dress in mourning and seek an audience with the king. Her story, told convincingly to David, was that one of her sons had slain the other, and the kinsmen were demanding the life of the murderer. Her sorrow, she explained, was that gaining vengeance for the dead son would cost the life of her remaining son. David rose to the occasion and vowed no harm would come to the surviving son—whereupon the woman pointed the finger at David for not fetching home his banished son, and uttered some of the most touching words of evangelism in the Old Testament: "For we must needs die, and are as water spilt on the ground, which cannot be gathered up again; neither doth God respect any person: yet doth he devise means, that his banished be not expelled from him" (2 Sam. 14:14).

And so Absalom was allowed to come home, although for two full years he and his father did not yet meet. And what have the past five years done to Absalom? They have brought to evil bloom the seeds of rebellion. He never had a father, he never had any restraints put on him, he had no yardstick by which to measure himself, he had no God, he had come home with a twisted view that today is the only day there is, and one must take what he wants. If he sounds like someone you know, remember we are looking into an eternal mirror.

While the son is groping for meaning in his life—the father, David, has retreated to his dream world. See his unreal view of his sons. He did nothing when Tamar was insulted; he does nothing now to bridge the chasm between his son and himself. By just letting his sons do whatever they wished, he fed the tendency toward sin.

Stealing Hearts to Steal a Throne

So, after four years of stealing the people's hearts and being unable to break into David's heart, Absalom made his move. He asked permission to go to Hebron to pray, thus keeping a vow he said he made in exile. David is relieved, no doubt, to see this evidence of religion, and gladly bids him go.

But Absalom posted spies on all the mountains south of Jerusalem with trumpets in their hands, and sent spies through all the land to say that when the trumpet sounded, "Absalom is king!" (v. 10, RSV). Two hundred of the choicest soldiers of the realm accompanied Absalom, not knowing the real purpose of the journey. The trumpets sounded, the people shouted, the crowds gathered on his path back to Jerusalem, and it seemed the throne was to be his.

Meanwhile, back at the palace, word of the rebellion had been brought to David. What a tragic scene then takes place, as David flees Jerusalem with little but the clothes on his back. See his tiny group as they hurry past the last house, through the city gate, over the brook Kidron, and up the Mount of Olives. Old and gray, barefoot and bent, scorned and weeping, David flees before Absalom. In this march of misfortune, one man even dares stand on a hillside and throw rocks at the king, calling him a man of the devil, and saying this has come upon him because of his sins. Where are those who used to shout, "Saul has slain his thousands; but David his ten thousands"? They are not here; they crowd the path of another, a younger man named Absalom.

Yet David gathers as he goes; old friends from years gone by come like ghosts out of the twilight to take their stand with their old commander—Ittai the Gittite among them, who makes that deathless declaration of love and loyalty: "As the Lord liveth, and as my Lord the king liveth, surely in what place my lord the king shall be, whether in death or life, even there also will thy servant be" (v. 21)

It was obvious that Absalom could not afford to let David live, and like a hound on the trail, he tracked David through the wilderness and across the Jordan until, in the wood of Ephraim, the old king had to make a stand and fight for his life. David divided his soldiers into three groups, putting over them Joab, Abishai, and Ittai. The war council of David and his generals was like no other in history—he commanded them that no harm should come to the enemy commander, Absalom!

And so the battle raged through the cool morning, and under the blazing noontime sun, and into the shadows of evening. Twenty thousand men perished in that battle to steal a father's throne. Late in the evening, a despairing Absalom was galloping through the woods when his hair became tangled in the lower limbs of a tree. While he dangled betwixt heaven and earth, one of Joab's men saw him and ran to tell his commander. Joab quickly gathered his weapons and his armor-bearers and raced to the scene, where he thrust his spears through Absalom's heart. The ten young men who bore Joab's armor then threw the body of the prince of Israel into a deep pit, and piled a heap of stones over him. Thus was the burial of the one who raised for himself a monument in the Vale of the Kings.

Twilight comes on, and a chill settles on these who have slain Absalom. The deed is done, and the news must now be borne to the father. David waits back at the little village behind the lines. Through the night he paces back and forth just within the gates. Up on the ramparts the watchman peers out into the dark. About dawn there is a cry from the wall, and the news is given that a runner comes. Then another. And soon the speck of dust on the horizon is a man banging at the gates, out of breath. David's first question and only interest is the welfare of Absalom, and the first runner, either out of ignorance or pity, gives no answer. The second runner is soon at the gate, and when the question is put to him he shows no hesitation: "The enemies of my lord the king, and all that rise against thee to do thee hurt, be as that young man is" (18:32).

I can see the king as he chokes back a cry, tears filling his eyes. He stumbles up the stairs to weep in solitude; but in the turning of the stairway there rises in the shadows the grim visage of one now gone, the prophet Nathan, whose bony finger reaches out of the gloom even now and whose voice is yet heard:

> [Thus saith the Lord,] Now therefore the sword shall never depart from thine house; because thou hast despised me, and hast taken the wife of Uriah the Hittite to be thy wife. . . . Behold, I will raise up evil against thee out of thine own house" (2 Sam. 12:10-11).

And the cry the people heard was that of a sinner man, the cry of a father who has killed his son, a cry of regret, remorse, and sorrow: "O my son Absalom, my son, my son Absalom! Would God I had died for thee, O Absalom, my son, my son!" (18:33).

The Refrain of Failure

Here is a father who failed. He was a great king but a poor father, from all the evidence. He forgot that admonition of Deuternomy about the Law of God:

> And thou shalt teach them diligently unto thy children, and

shalt talk of them when thou sittest in thine house, and when thou walkest by the way, and when thou liest down, and when thou risest up (Deut. 6:7).

I heard about a hog at one of our state fairs a few years ago. That hog was about all that a hog ought to be. His hair was parted in the middle and nicely combed. His hooves were manicured in such a fashion as to have roused the envy of a movie star. Everybody who saw the hog realized that the man who raised him knew his business. Now, the boy who was set to look after this hog seemed to have been chosen to further emphasize the beauty of the hog. He was a little wizen-faced, hollow-chested, hatchet-heeled fellow who seemed bent upon burning up all the cigarettes in the world as quick as he could.

But the startling fact about the whole situation is that the owner of the hog and the father of the boy were the same man! In the hog business the man was a roaring success, but in the boy-raising business he was an utter failure![1]

Here is a son who failed. He failed his father—he never really gave him a chance to change. He failed his God—he apparently never had any real relationship to God. He never realized that God has no grandsons; each of us has to build his own relationship to God.

He failed himself. He should have been the next king of Israel; Solomon became king only by accident. Absalom was the heir apparent. He saw his glory fade and die, a glory which should have been greater than that of Solomon.

Absalom should have had a monarch's funeral—the rich and the poor should have come to kneel together at the bier of the great king and praise God for his wisdom and love like unto that of his father David. He should have had a soldier's funeral, borne to his final resting place amid the stirring roll of drums and the sunlight flashing on the shields of a thousand soldiers who wept unashamedly. Instead, the mangled body of the most illustrious prince of Israel was cast like the carcass of a dead lion into a pit, with only the jackals to howl his passing.

On moonlit nights surely David often went to the Vale of the Kings to sit at the monument Absalom raised for himself, and to weep at what might have been but never was. And any who chanced by could hear the melancholy cry, "O, my son Absalom . . . would God I had died for thee!"

David couldn't die for his son. You can't die for your son, either. But Jesus did. For God has indeed, through the cross of Jesus, "devised means that his banished be not expelled from him."

No matter how you as a father have failed, God will forgive you, and give you the new heart needed to be a good and righteous father, a father your wife and children can be proud of, a father who can be followed as a godly example. For the blood of Jesus covers all the sins of any repentant heart.

If you have failed as a son or daughter, hear me carefully. You are not in an everlasting exile from your Heavenly Father. He wants to forgive you, He wants to welcome you into His family. There is a great emphasis these days on bringing runaway youth back home. The billboards say you can call home free; the advertisements say you can ride the bus back home free, even if it's across the nation.

Listen, my teenage friend, God loves you so much that Jesus died for your runaway angers and fears and rebellions.

And you can come back from wherever your banished heart may be—whether on drugs, or alcohol, or sex, or feeling like a failure—the salvation Jesus offers on His cross will bring you home.

5
A Salvation We Can Understand
Ephesians 2:1-10

For by grace are ye saved through faith (Eph. 2:8).

We understand what a friend at church means when he says to us, "Save me a place at your table for Wednesday night supper." He wants us to lay claim to a place at our table for him. When we read that a certain boxer was "saved by the bell," we don't for a moment think that a bell ran up and saved him from anything—we know that the bell signaling the end of the round rang just in the nick of time. Every town has its salvage companies—junkyards we called them when I was growing up—which find a purpose for wrecked and apparently useless things. These are some of the ways we use the word *save*.

But the most profound use of the idea of salvation is in our religious life—when we speak of deliverance from evil; of our reconciliation with God; of our sense of security and purpose.

Man: " 'E Wobbles"

A little boy wanted to be an artist. His teenage brother came up one day and noticed him drawing a picture. Watching a moment, the brother pointed out that a man in the picture had two right arms. He remarked, "He'd look better if he had one right and one left arm." But the little boy replied, "I don't like everybody I draw to look right. Real people don't." And they don't! All of us have our problems, and the need for salvation is present in everybody's life. We need salvation because of our nature, because of the way we naturally are: we are a paradox, a problem to ourselves and to God. As G. A. Studdert-Kennedy, "Woodbine Willie" of World War I, said in his poem "Sinner and Saint," which describes the British soldier of that war:

> Our Padre, 'e says I'm a sinner,
>   And *John Bull* says I'm a saint,
> And they're both of 'em bound to be liars,
>   For I'm neither of them, I ain't.
> I'm a man, and a man's a mixture,
>   Right down from 'is very birth,
> For part ov 'im comes from 'eaven,
>   And part ov 'im comes from earth.
> There's nothing in man that's perfect,
>   And nothing that's all complete;
> 'E's nubbat a big beginning,
>   From 'is 'ead to the soles of 'is feet.
> There's sommat as draws 'im uppards,
>   And summat as drags 'im down,
> And the consekence is, 'e wobbles,
>   'Twixt muck and a golden crown.[1]

We need salvation because we are indeed a paradox, a mystery, a problem. We are made of the dust of the earth, and have so much in common with the animal world. But we have been breathed upon by God, and we're different from any other of His creation—we are a mystery. But we are a problem, a paradox—there is a tension between that part of us which strains toward heaven and that part of us which is of the earth, earthy. Part of our problem is that we have forgotten why God created us. We have forgotten that we are to be stewards. We have forgotten that our dominion over all the earth is to be under His dominion.

The paradox is seen in that, while we are God's crowning work of creation, we have torn aside those ties that bind us to God and we stand over against Him in opposition to His will. This willful rebellion against God in every life has caused tragedy, sorrow, sickness, death, broken relationships, lack of purpose, lack of security—and we are doing it to ourselves! Why? The Bible asserts we are killing ourselves with our sins because we were born with a tendency to choose evil over good, and we feed that tendency.

We were born with a desire to promote self over God. We love, in our twisted pride, to "lord" it over both man and God. If we could only keep the truth of the dramatic funeral speech made in 1715 by Bishop Massillon at the funeral of Louis XIV, of France, who called himself "The Great."

His body, dressed in the richest robes, rested in a golden coffin. To emphasize his greatness, orders had been given that, instead of the thousands of candles one would expect on such an occasion, the cathedral should be lighted by a single candle. Flickering in the semidarkness, it cast a softly shimmering light on the gleaming coffin.

Thousands had crowded into the place. The hushed silence was broken only by their sobs. Then, in a moment of extraordinary drama, Jean Baptiste Massillon, the revered cleric, rose to speak. His oration, which has echoed down the centuries, consisted of only four words. Slowly reaching down from the pulpit, he snuffed out the lone candle, saying: "Only God is great!"

But listen—as dark and powerful as sin is, it is not the ultimate fact. For standing over against this reality of sin is God's gracious salvation in Jesus Christ. And that's the final word!

Let's spend the next few minutes considering a question about salvation to which there is no answer. In Hebrews 2:3-4, we find a very sobering question:

> *How shall we escape, if we neglect so great salvation;* which at the first began to be spoken by the Lord, and was confirmed unto us by them that heard him; God also bearing them witness, both with signs and wonders, and with divers miracles, and gifts of the Holy Ghost, according to his own will? (Author's italics).

There is no escape if we neglect so great salvation! No escape from the ravages of sin; no escape from the schemes of the devil; no escape from eternal separation from God.

All the more reason we should give careful ear to the proclaiming of this wonderful salvation. One of the clearest ways to understand so great salvation as that offered by Christ is to use the striking organization suggested by Dale Moody: the one way of salvation; the two sides of salvation; and the three dimensions of salvation.[2]

The One Way of Salvation

One of the most stirring stories of the early Christians is the account in Acts 4 of the imprisonment of Peter and John for preaching the resurrection of the dead through Jesus. The authorities arrested Peter and John and flung them into prison—a bit late, since about five thousand men believed through the preaching of that day! The Jewish religious leaders gathered on the next day to grill the two disciples, and opened the door for Peter to witness by asking, "By what power, or by what name, have ye done this?" (v. 7). Here, in verses 9 through 12, is Peter's reply, a classic.

> If we this day be examined of the good deed done to the impotent man, by what means he is made whole; Be it known unto you all, and to all the people of Israel, that by the name of Jesus Christ of Nazareth, whom ye crucified, whom God raised from the dead, even by him doth this man stand here before you whole. This is the stone which was set at nought of you builders, which is become the head of the corner. Neither is there salvation in any other: for there is none other name under heaven given among men, whereby we must be saved.

And in the sixteenth chapter of Acts we find Paul and Silas in Philippi, preaching. A slave girl follows after them, crying: "These men are the servants of the most high God, which shew unto us the way of salvation" (v. 17). Paul cast the spirit of divination out of the distraught girl, and her masters, seeing their goose and golden eggs were departed, raised such a hue and cry that Paul and Silas were imprisoned.

You know the familiar story of the singing at midnight in the dungeon, the earthquake, and the fearful jailer's rushing in to find the prisoners all safe. Then his question to Paul and Silas: "Sirs, what must I do to be saved?" And the answer comes ringing: "Believe on the Lord Jesus" (vv. 30-31).

The Bible doesn't generalize, it doesn't camouflage, it doesn't cover up—*there is only one way for people under*

God's wrath to be saved! No salvation is possible by general religion, no salvation by good works, no salvation through your education or your friends: without Christ, "the soul that sinneth; it shall die!"

Paul beautifully expresses this truth in our text, Ephesians 2:1-10, saying that there is no salvation for sinful persons except through the grace and mercy of God.

> Could my tears forever flow,
> Could my zeal no languor know,
> These for sin could not atone;
> Thou must save, and Thou alone:
> In my hand no price I bring,
> Simply to Thy cross I cling.

The Two Sides to Salvation

The two sides to salvation: God's grace and man's faith. I remember an incident during my first days as pastor in Memphis. My wife and I were the guests at one of the ladies' Sunday School class meetings. As we had refreshments, the folks around the circle, one by one, told us about themselves. Finally we came to the only man in the group besides myself, the husband of the hostess. He stated his situation accurately and succinctly: "My name is Gene Dinstuhl, and I was saved by grace some thirty years ago!" What I at first mistook for a theological statement was clarified in the group laughter—his wife's name is Grace!

Truly, all of us Christians have all been saved by grace. God has freely done for each of us through Christ that which we could not do for ourselves. Grace means gift, and God gave us the gift of Christ, and through Him we have been given inner peace, freedom, and cleansing from sin.

Salvation is something God had to do for us. Salvation is a free gift God holds out, and yet *it is not ours until we will reach out and receive it.* When I am away for speaking engagements, I usually bring back a gift for my wife. Recently, I got on the airplane with a rather large gift, beautifully wrapped and tied with a big ribbon bow. I think every flight attendant on the plane asked for it! But I would have been very disappointed if my wife had showed no interest in it and would not accept it. So the gift of salvation must be accepted on our part for the work of Christ to be effective.

Inward trust in Jesus as God's answer to sin is the only proper response for you and me to make to the cross. And this response is more than intellect; it is more than passive acceptance of facts. Nobody fully understands salvation—but then, what air traveler fully understands all the dynamics of jet propulsion? It works, and that we do know.

Outward confession, as Paul urges in Romans 10:9-10, is the natural—no, make that supernatural—response of the person who has experienced salvation. Only through the presence and guidance of the Holy Spirit can we realize our sin, experience godly sorrow, and be led to repentance. Only by the Holy Spirit are we to turn from our love of sin and turn to a loving God, receiving forgiveness. At every step of the way, the two sides of salvation go hand-in-hand: the grace of God, and the faith of man.

The Three Dimensions of Salvation

There is an instructive story, often told about the great Greek scholar, Bishop B. F. Westcott, which helps us see the three dimensions of our salvation. One day as the Bishop was out for a walk, a Salvation Army lass approached him with the question, "Sir, are you saved?" The scholar in Westcott came to the surface as, full of his knowledge of Greek tenses, he replied, "Which do you mean—have I *been* saved, am I *being* saved, or *will* I *be saved* in the future?"

Savlation does have its three tenses—*past, present,* and *future.* A *past* reality with its removal of the penalty and guilt of sin; a *present* reality with its removal of the overwhelming power of sin, though we still wrestle with the dark force daily; and a *future* reality with its freedom from the very presence and existence of sin.

There is a sense in which we should speak, as the Salvation Army girl did, of our *past* salvation. We Baptists come down hard on this aspect. As we look back on that time when we accepted Christ, we want to stress the new person in Christ, that glorious change we call *regeneration.* The wages of sin are nullified; there is no longer a fearful looking for judgment; our sins are nailed to the cross. This is what happens as soon as a person repents and invites Jesus into his or her heart. If you have been saved even one hour, then you can look back and speak of your salvation in the past tense, saying, "Thank God—I have been saved!" An example of this emphasis is found in our text, Ephesians 2:1-10, in verse 5, in which Paul uses a Greek perfect participle, with the force of a past event in whose influence you continue to stand: "By grace you *are* saved" (author's italics)—have been and continue to be in that state!

> At the cross, at the cross where I first saw the light,
> And the burden of my heart rolled away,

> It was there by faith I received my sight,
> And now I am happy all the day!

While that hour when we "walk the aisle" deserves to have a special place in our hearts, we must remember that there is a fuller dimension of our salvation.

Salvation is much more than a past event, a debt paid on our behalf, a transaction affecting our eternal welfare. The *present-tense* understanding of our salvation stresses the *unfolding new relationship* we have to God as His children— the increasing difference between our lives, and our desires, and the world's way. This emphasis upon the ongoing work of salvation in our lives is often called *sanctification.*

In 1 Corinthians 1:18 we find a good example of our "being saved." Paul says: "For the word of the cross is folly to those who are perishing, but to us who are *being saved* it is the power of God" (RSV, author's italics). Here Paul uses the Greek present participle.

In Philippians 2:12-13, Paul admonishes the members of that church to "work out your own salvation with fear and trembling. For it is God which worketh in you both to will and to do of his good pleasure." God works the salvation in; the Christian must work it out!

The present tense idea of salvation stresses two things: the *being set apart*—and realizing it—from the world as God's own people, God's special treasure, and the *responsibility to grow spiritually* in the likeness of Christ. There is a heavy emphasis in Paul's writings upon not remaining spiritual babes, but growing in wisdom and understanding. The hymn by Charles Wesley, "Love Divine, All Loves Excelling" expresses this aspect well:

> Finish, then, thy new creation;
> Pure and spotless let us be;
> Let us see thy great salvation
> Perfectly restored in thee.
> Changed from glory into glory,
> Till in heaven we take our place,
> Till we cast our crowns before thee,
> Lost in wonder, love, and praise.

The third of the dimensions of our salvation is vividly seen in Romans 13:11 where Paul tells the Romans their salvation is nearer than when they first believed. And Peter makes a remarkable statement about this future aspect of our salvation in 1 Peter 1:5 as he describes the Christians as those "Who are kept by the power of God through faith unto salvation ready to be revealed in the last time."

Peter here speaks of a full and complete salvation to be revealed in heaven. It is a promise of *glorification,* which is possible only when we are free from the very presence of sin. Full and future salvation can be described by the hope of the glory of everlasting life, the joy of being in the presence of God and with our friends, and the total absence of sin.

No more sin! William Barclay has a haunting story of the man who had sailed the seas for decades and had grown weary at heart and desperately wanted to escape the bondage of the deep. So he put an oar on his shoulder and set out to journey inland over moor and mountain until he came to a land where the people would stare and ask what that strange thing was he carried on his shoulder.[3]

That is exactly what we look forward to in the future tense of salvation—a land where those happy folk know nothing more of the horrors of sin.

Salvation: only one way, but two necessary sides to it. Salvation: three dimensions to be tasted, enjoyed, possessed—past, present, future. I have been saved from the penalty of sin, praise God! I am being daily saved from the power of sin and becoming more like my Lord, praise God! I shall be saved one day when I stand before Him—saved from the very presence of sin.

One man said it took him forty years to learn three things: First, that he couldn't do anything to save himself; second, that God didn't require him to do anything to save himself; and third, that Jesus had already done all that was necessary to save him. It took a long time, but it was priceless.

> And when, before the throne,
> I stand in Him complete,
> "Jesus died my soul to save,"
> My lips shall still repeat.

6
What Is Special in Christianity?
2 Corinthians 5:14-21

Therefore if any man be in Christ, he is a new creature: old things are passed away; behold, all things are become new (2 Cor. 5:17).

What is special in Christianity? Let us not think it idle speculation to ask such a question in an evangelical church service, for there are many questioning folks in every congregation.

What is special? Certainly it is not our belief in a god. Hindus worship Brahma; Zoroastrians hail Ahura Mazda as their supreme being; Buddhism, while originally without a divine being, has come to worship its founder; Muslims claim Allah; and Jews call upon Jehovah.

What is special? It is not the emphasis upon morality in Christianity, for who among us has not been impressed with the harsh, but moral, commandments of Islam as we have been exposed to it on national television?

What is special? However marvelous the special revelation in the Bible is, it is not our main mark of uniqueness, for other world religions have their sacred writings. The Hindu reads the Vedas; the Zoroastrian studies the Avesta; Taoism has its book, the Tao-Te Ching; and the Muslim can even show you the name of Jesus in his Koran.

What, Then, Is Special in Christianity?

It is this man Jesus. He is the unmistakable, irreplaceable, definite center of the Christian faith. He is the ultimate measure of the Christian's walk, the ultimate hope of the Christian's life.

Christianity is not synonymous, as some would have it, with truth, beauty, love. These things only take on their Christian meaning as they have explicit reference to the man Jesus, who is the Christ. Likewise, there can be no anonymous Christianity, nor an anonymous Christian. By nature, there must be identification with the man Jesus.

It is so easy to speak of Jesus, but which Jesus is for real? We all read the same Bible, and yet there are so many ideas of Jesus. There is Albert Schweitzer's apocalyptic rabbi in the lurid and sulphurous light of a cosmic catastrophe, who seizes the spokes of the grinding wheel of the world to set it moving toward the kingdom of God and is himself caught upon it and hangs there throughout the ages.[1]

There is the caricature of Jesus in an ad found in an "underground" magazine: Dresses poorly. Said to be a carpenter by trade. Ill-nourished, has visionary ideas, associates with common working people, the unemployed and bums. Alien—believed to be a Jew. Professional Agitator, Red Beard, marks on hands and feet the results of injuries inflicted by an angry mob led by respectable citizens.[2]

There is Bruce Barton's *Man Nobody Knows,* in His gray pinstripe suit, the founder of modern business. These differences should not bother us, because even the writers of the four Gospels, not to mention Paul, did not see Him exactly from the same perspective. It simply means that in the New Testament we do not have objective biographies,

WHAT IS SPECIAL IN CHRISTIANITY?

but rather profound testimonies of His power by overwhelmed and inspired followers. And those folks all held a united basic faith in Jesus as Lord and Savior. What, then, does it mean to say that Jesus is the central point in the Christian religion?

Jesus: The Part of God You Can See

That's the way a little child answered the question: "Who is Jesus?"—"The part of God you can see!" And those who saw Jesus in the flesh saw a real person. He is no fable, no myth. He is a historical figure, and more is known of him than of the leader of any other world religion. He has been studied more than any other figure in history, and Mary's fears as portrayed in the play, "Family Portrait," are unfounded: she stumbled on through life after the cruel crucifixion of her son, and when a child is born in Nazareth to her youngest son Judah, she shyly asks him to name the boy Jesus. When pressed for her reason, she smiles wanly, fools with her apron a moment, and softly says, "because I would not have him to be forgotten!" As she lights a candle and turns to the window, there is music, and the long shadow of the crucified falls upon all the earth.[3]

To be sure, God will always be a large mystery to us; but as far as we can tell, he was like this preaching carpenter. "The part of God you can see." "Immanuel: God with us." God *in the flesh,* revealing God in eternity. God *confined* to time and space; the Maker of heaven and earth confined to a human body, and to the tiny country of Palestine. God *at work,* on a scale to which we could see and respond. God *identifying* with man in our plight, leading us out of the maze. The Arabs challenged T. E. Lawrence, "if you would lead us, you must eat our food, sleep in our shelters, take our risks, shoulder our responsibility, live our life—and do it better than we!"

Men have always marveled at the depth of His humanity. They looked back and marveled: He was God and yet so like us; His enemies charged he ate and drank with sinners. He grew weary and sat on the well of John 4. He said to the man lowered through the roof: "Child, God is not angry with you," yet He grew angry with the money changers; He wept at Lazarus's tomb and agonized in the garden. Those who were closest remembered no aloof, stained-glass saint— yet His humanity is the model for every Christian.

The other side of the coin: "Like as we are, yet without sin." The realization of Jesus' Deity came slowly and was built on three things: what He said, what He did, and the resurrection. He said that when men saw Him they saw God—that God is, through all eternity, what this man was in His thirty-three years among us. He did things that, in themselves, raised questions about who He was. But the resurrection was the crowning proof of Jesus' special, different relationship to God. Today, we cannot see Him, or see Him do mighty miracles, but we have the inner witness of the Holy Spirit and the inspired Word of God.

Why Did Jesus Come to Earth?

The unanimous testimony of the Bible is that Jesus came to set men free from the burden of sin: "God was in Christ, reconciling the world unto himself." Genesis 1—11 sets forth the terrible plight of mankind, staggering through time and eternity, carrying a hijacked freedom humanity cannot handle. A freedom God never equipped man to handle, a freedom that feeds upon its own lust and self-love and falls prey to the devil.

And the sad result of this flawed and doomed rebellion against our Maker is that every person has gone astray. Not all the good deeds or kind hearts in all the world can suffice to gain salvation, a way home to God. Christ did something for us we could not do for ourselves. My old college roommate used to tell a story which illustrates the emptiness of our efforts to save ourselves, to put out the fires of hell which rage within.

In the little village where he was pastor there was only a volunteer fire department. So, when the fire bell rang all the able-bodied men ran for the garage which served as the fire station, jumped in or on the dilapidated old fire truck, which went screaming to the fire. Now, on this old vehicle, a couple of men had to pump up the pressure of the water tank by hand pumps on the way to the fire. So imagine the scene as the old truck is rumbling down the road, bell clanging, light flashing, siren screaming, men on the back pumping, one man with the nozzle of the fire hose in hand so they could jump off as soon as the truck came screeching to a halt at the fire.

On this particular morning, racing to the fire—wouldn't you know it?—the brakes failed! So they came around the curve, the burning house right there by the side of the road, but the truck couldn't stop! Helpless to do more, the man sprayed the water as they raced on by! Our efforts to save ourselves are every bit as futile! All of us have gone astray and live under the judgment of God. We are damned and doomed if we are without Christ. So Jesus came to earth to rescue wandering sinners and lead them home to heaven.

How Does Jesus Save People?

In a very unexpected way! In answer to why Jesus came to earth, a child said: "Jesus came and did something we didn't expect Him to do." As a matter of fact, He did two things we didn't expect Him to do. First, He died on a cross as a common criminal for our sins, and secondly, He was raised from the grave on the third day.

It was only after the resurrection that His followers began to ponder the cross: If He is God, then why the horrible cross? And many folks today stop right here; the cross is a stumbling block. They can see Jesus as a good man, yes, but Jesus as a God who died on a cross, no. The eternal significance of the cross is greater than anyone can nail down, and beginning with the New Testament writers, people have pondered it for twenty centuries.

The New Testament writers gave us several word pictures in trying to convey the meaning of the cross. *Sacrifice* is a key word for understanding the death of Jesus. In the Old Testament sacrificial system, once a year the sins of the people were symbolically laid on a "scapegoat" which was then driven out of the camp. Thus we see the transfer of the guilt from the guilty to the innocent, and that is what the cross is all about. For there the innocent died for your sins and mine.

Sometimes the meaning of the cross is seen in the idea of a *ransom*. He came, He said, to give His life a ransom for many. A ransom is usually a price paid to someone to redeem someone else. To whom was Christ's life paid as a ransom? Some folks say the ransom of Christ's life was paid as a ransom to the devil—an idea many other folks reject with good reason. God is not held in ransom! No, there is no reference in the Bible to paying any ransom to the devil; and all parents know that there is so much heartache and brokenness in this world that demands giving in order to bring healing. The ransom is just paid.

Often we seek to shed light on the meaning of the cross by using Paul's *legal terminology*. We say God is the Judge, man is the guilty one, and Jesus takes our place when the sentence is passed. This is known as justification, best defined as God, on account of Jesus' death, looking on me just as if I had never sinned. Jesus died in my place, for my sins. Again, a child's answer: "Jesus let Himself be crucified so His friends wouldn't be crucified." The predicament was so terrible, the love was so great, that the only way was the way of the cross.

About the cross, while no person plumbs its depth, we can say some things with certainty. It was on behalf of each of us—He *did for us what we could never do for ourselves,* removing the penalty and condemnation of sin. The cross was *not an accident,* an incidental, inevitable collision of Jesus with the Jewish and Roman authorities—it was a *voluntary* sacrifice on His part; the reason He came to earth. The cross is the *grounds on which our sins are forgiven.* The cross, and it alone, is the bridge from our sins to God. The cross is the *climax of our revelation about God.*

How Should I Respond to Jesus?

First, by opening your heart to the truth about Him as you find it in the Bible, in the lives of Christian friends, and in the proclamation of the gospel by the church. The Bible and the inner witness of the Holy Spirit say that love so amazing, so divine, demands and deserves your life's allegiance. This truth was vividly brought home to me some years ago when my son, Deryl, was about four years old. We were going somewhere in the car. Suddenly, out of the blue he turned to me and asked, "Daddy, does God love us?" I smiled and assured him that God loved us and sent Jesus to invite us to live with Him in heaven. This seemed to satisfy him for a few moments, then he turned again and asked, "Daddy, *why* does God love us?" I didn't have the answer to that one, having often wondered myself why God puts up with this rebellious creation. But I talked of God's loving His children and assured him again that God loves us. He was quiet for perhaps five minutes, and then posed, in earnestness, this question: "Daddy, do we love God?" Do we?

If we truly love God, a part of the commitment of our lives to Jesus is turning away from our sins—the decision that Jesus is more worthy of our love than our old habits, our old loves, and our old lusts. That means we have to trust Jesus. Again, a child described how he trusted Jesus: "If I asked Jesus if He liked me, He probably wouldn't answer me—He would probably send me another kid to play with—He does things like that." That is an example of trust: are you willing to believe, like that child, that Jesus really does want you to be happy, and is going to do what is best for you?

Another part of trust is to believe that Jesus is interested in daily communion with us. Another child put it like this: "When I talk to Jesus, He bends down to me." And so He does. The big question is whether you will look up to Him in repentance and faith. If you will, He will reach down.

7
Coats and Christianity
Mark 10:46-52

And immediately he received his sight, and followed Jesus in the way (Mark 10:52).

I visited her soon after becoming her pastor and, to be honest, expected to find the visit depressing, for she was blind, and had been for many years. But far from being down and focusing on what most of us would call a misfortune, she was a cheerful, independent person.

Have you ever pondered what it is like to be blind? I remember visiting Mammoth Cave years ago and having the lights turned off by the guide. The darkness was so dark you could almost feel it, and eyes were absolutely useless! How warm and friendly the light was when the switch was thrown and the floodlights changed the abyss back into a fairyland!

"I am blind and it is May." That sign, hung around the neck of a blind beggar, speaks to me vividly. There is so much to see, to experience in this lovely world. To be blind physically is not to know the beauty of the sunrise or see the stately wheeling of the battalion of ducks coming in to land on a pond or revel in the colors of the extravagant carpet of summer flowers on a mountainside.

Helen Keller, so brave and inspiring in her blindness and deafness, once wrote a magazine article entitled "Three

Days to See," in which she outlined what she as a blind person would do if she could have three days of sight. It was a powerful and thought-provoking article. Toward the end she made this statement: "I who am blind can give one hint to those who see: Use your eyes as if tomorrow you would be stricken blind."[1] What a challenging thought!

Yet, there are worse kinds of blindness than physical loss of our sight. An old saying puts it bluntly: "None are so blind as those who will not see." The most terrible kind of blindness is spiritual blindness, which leads to eternal darkness.

There is the spiritual blindness to the Word of God. Mark Twain, who is not my favorite guide in religious matters, nevertheless put his finger on this terrible blindness when he commented, "It is not those parts of the Bible that I cannot understand that give me trouble. It is those clear passages that I *can* understand and do nothing about that haunt me!"

There is the spiritual blindness to God's love. How tragic it is to spend half of one's life and not know of God's love for us! How doubly tragic it is to let three score and ten years go by without getting acquainted with God. The daughter of Mark Twain described the spiritual blindness of many in her comment when her father one day received an invitation to an audience with some foreign potentate. "Gracious, Daddy," she declared, "At this rate you'll soon be acquainted with everybody but God!" How sad, but how true of many.

There is the spiritual blindness to God's salvation. How pathetic it is to see the spiritually blind groping their way through this world, refusing to see spiritually; putting their hands over their eyes, ostrich-like, in the matter of salvation. We go through life tense, anxious, and worried about many things, really trying to be our own saviors, and when it is all over and done with—we are aware that we have no more confidence in our own ability to save ourselves than the country farmer had in the airplane. When asked about his first ride, he replied with a drawl, "Waal, it's all right, I guess, but the contraption was so flimsy that I was afraid to put my weight down the whole time I was up there!" Many are blind to the plain salvation Jesus offers, knowing life is but a vapor, ignoring the truth of God's Word, but scared to put our weight down on the philosophies of the world.

A Man Born Blind

Listen to the story of a blind man who wasn't blind to the deepest truths in life. His name was Bartimaeus, the son of Timaeus. Bartimaeus was born blind. He never saw the singing bird, the purple-and-golden glory of the lilies of the field, or experienced the silent thunder of the sunrise. *He was blind.*

He sat by the roadside, day after day, begging. I have strolled along the Wadi Kelt among the ruins of Herod's winter palace in New Testament Jericho, and tried to picture in my mind's eye the road where blind Bartimaeus sat. He was brought there early, perhaps by some neighbors or relatives on their way to work each day. You can imagine how quickly the hot sun in Jericho began to beat down on him, and how uncomfortable he would become each day. Like another beggar in one of Jesus' parables, he may have suffered from disease and sores, and waged a hard battle with the village dogs.

The world went by, unseeing and uncaring. What was one beggar, more or less? He *heard* the sounds of camels, the shouts of children, the gossip of women, the business talk of passing men, the rustling of the wind in the palms and the rolling claps of thunder—but he *saw* nothing. *He was blind.*

He had long ago spent what little money he or his family may have had, in a vain search for sight. If he had gotten well, gained his sight, his family and friends would have rejoiced with him; had he died, the same folks would have mourned his passing—but he did neither. He simply sat there, day after day. *Blind.*

His hope of ever gaining his sight was almost gone, yet like a drowning man, he grasped at any and every straw. There was the prophet Jesus from Nazareth, who had a growing reputation of being able to heal the blind, the lame, and the deaf. True, Jesus hardly fit the description of a great man—a carpenter, a preacher of a strange gospel of turning the other cheek, but beggars can't be choosy! Nor did he quite fit the passage of Scripture Bartimaeus had memorized long ago and now only mumbled, or half sang in a singsong style as he squatted in the broiling sun and begged:

> I the Lord have called thee in righteousness, and will hold thine hand, and will keep thee, and give thee for a covenant of the people, for a light of the Gentiles; To open the blind eyes, to bring out the prisoners from the prison, and them that sit in darkness out of the prison house. (Isa. 42:6).

Then one day the news he was waiting for came! Maybe a friend told him, or perhaps he picked it up from passing conversation between two women on their way to market. However it happened, it put Bartimaeus's pulse racing, and plans began to form in his mind about how he would accomplish his daring idea.

Panting and full of fear, in strange surroundings and on a strange street, nevertheless Bartimaeus was ready. This was the street, this was the hour, the noise and commotion around told Bartimaeus that Jesus was coming down the street—it was now or never!

In a high, wavering voice he screamed out. Have you ever heard an old man scream at the top of his lungs? Those folks around the blind beggar rebuked him—"Shut up, old man—can't you see the prophet is talking with the mayor?" But the more they yelled at him to be silent, the more the old beggar screamed out—"Jesus, thou son of David, have mercy on me!"

> Pass me not, O gentle Savior,
> Hear my humble cry;
> While on others thou art calling,
> Do not pass me by.
>
> —Fanny J. Crosby

And then Jesus saw him, and stood still, and commanded that they bring Bartimaeus to Him. Do you suppose it was Peter that Jesus sent to get Bartimaeus? At any rate, ponder with me the amazing fact that the blind man saw himself, though blind!

The Blind Man Saw Himself

How wonderful that this blind man could see himself! He needed no eye specialist to tell him that he was in bad shape! If only we could see our spiritual sickness as plainly as he saw his physical need. If only we were as determined to reach the Great Physician with our spiritual illness as he was to contact this man who could heal blind eyes! What a tragedy that we so often fail to ask for help.

Just this past week, my bedside phone rang at three AM. When I picked up the receiver, I heard sobbing. When I said, "Hello," the sobbing continued for a moment, then there was a click, and the line went dead. Someone with a need, hurting terribly, had gotten up the courage to call a minister. But at the last moment, when he or she heard my voice, the fear, the shame, the confusion was too much. Perhaps, just perhaps, I could have guided this hurting person to the Great Physician. I will never know. Only God knows the broken hearts and shattered dreams and lives in any town—or in any congregation. "O what peace we often forfeit, O what needless pain we bear, all because we do not carry everything to God in prayer."

So often folks remind me of a story my father used to enjoy, being an insurance salesman. It seems the policyholder had died, and the insurance agent was making a routine call at the home to fill out the necessary forms. The wife was quite ignorant of such matters, and growing fearful at the questions concerning the death, reassured the agent that "it warn't nothing serious" that killed her husband!

Sin gnaws away at our spiritual vitals. Our consciences finally cease to beg for our attention, and we sit hopeless in our darkness. Not so this beggar, Bartimaeus. He stopped shrugging and saying, "Tomorrow." He began to realize that it was *today* that he needed Christ.

Greater Than the Sun Standing Still

Notice another thing. This beggar commanded a greater miracle to happen than Joshua's halting of the sun in its gallop across the skies. Bartimaeus caused Jesus to stand still! Jesus didn't have a planned meeting with this beggar, no three o'clock appointment at the curb of Dead Sea Drive and Roman Road Circle. The truth of the matter is that Jesus was on His way to the cross—fifteen miles to go to the Holy City—but He stopped for a blind beggar.

Jesus did that all the time. He never seemed to become as busy as you and me. The woman who touched the hem of His robe, the widow who was burying her only son and met Jesus in the road, the demoniac in the middle of the night, the woman at the well—none of these were planned appointments. Jesus had time to listen, to care, to witness, to help. I know that He has time for you this very day.

Call the Blind Man!

I sometimes wish that the Bible were not so brutally honest about our human nature. Look how the crowd responded to Jesus' command to bring the blind man. Suddenly he who was only a bag of trash, a nuisance underfoot, now became a real person. He had plenty of help now. "Come, Bartimaeus, hurry, He's calling for you! Here's Peter, he'll take you to Jesus!" Most helpful, they were!

The old man struggled unsteadily to his feet, stumbled a moment over his ragged old coat, wrestled with it—and threw it aside.

And what's true of old coats must be true also of our

sins, our pride, and our guilt. If you would come to Jesus, you must fling aside "the sin that doth so easily beset us."

I've thought about what must have raced through his mind as all those helping hands pulled him to his feet and he felt himself being guided toward the Master. It was really beyond belief, beyond understanding. But that didn't keep Bartimaeus from coming to Jesus. We don't need to understand the inner workings of salvation nearly as much as we simply need to accept it.

Are You Sure You Want Healing?

It seems strange that Jesus would ask a man obviously blind what he wanted from Him. Yet Jesus seems to have done that often; remember how he asked the man who had been paralyzed for thirty-eight years if he really wanted to be healed! I learned long ago that people often do not want to be helped or healed. Maybe it's due to our stubborn, sinful nature, or maybe our guilt has such a grip on us that we do not wish to face it, or maybe we are afraid to start all over, or maybe we're comfortable with the old rut, even if it's killing us!

Would you like for Jesus to change your life right now? Would you do what this blind beggar did—determine that you want out of your spiritual darkness? Will you do whatever you can to meet Jesus, as he did? When you feel the Spirit moving closer to you, will you back away or call out all the more loudly? Are you willing to cast away any and all hindrances to coming closer to Jesus? Will you face your spiritual problem and tell Jesus what you want?

The telling point of the story is that *Bartimaeus had not become reconciled* to the life of darkness. Nor must we!

"Lord, that I may receive my sight!" And then Jesus said those words worth worlds to hear—"Go thy way; thy faith hath made thee whole. And immediately he received his sight, and followed Jesus in the way."

No mass cure, no long line of people—just a blind beggar. A single miracle of grace and faith. But mark it well; Bartimaeus was no isolated wanderer in the land of darkness. There are many people, perhaps you among them, who yearn in their hearts for a meeting with Jesus, for a wonderful place . . .

> I wish there was some wonderful place
> Called the Land of Beginning Again,
> Where all our mistakes and all our heartaches,
> And all our selfish griefs
> Could be dropped at the door like a shabby old coat,
> And never put on again.
>
> —Louise Fletcher Tarkington

There is such a wonderful place, a land of beginning again. Right here where you are, right now as you are.

8
The Daring Young Man
Acts 13:13

Aristarchus . . . Marcus . . . and Justus. . . . These only are my fellow workers unto the kingdom of God, which have been a comfort unto me (Col. 4:10-11).

Several years ago, shortly after beginning a new pastorate, I decided to fulfill a childhood dream, that of learning to fly an airplane. For several months I studied aerodynamics, characteristics of the Piper Cherokee (a single-engine, low-winged aircraft), flight regulations, and weather information. We practiced stalls, simulated forced landings, touch-and-go landings, and a thousand other essentials to flight.

Then came the day I both desired and dreaded. After a series of touch and goes, the instructor said to me, "Do you think you can fly this thing?" What can any American male reply to that except, "Sure!" Motioning over to the taxiway the instructor said, "Well, let me out over there, and you take her around a couple of times!"

I taxied over and let my instructor out, then taxied out to the end of the runway. There I stopped for the customary preflight check of the plane—and to pray! And did I ever pray! "Lord, you didn't bring me to this city to rack it all up at the end of this runway!" I called the tower on the radio: "Tower, this is triple three fox, ready for takeoff on 17." I secretly hoped that either my radio wasn't working or the tower's wouldn't! No luck: "Triple three fox, you're cleared for takeoff."

I swallowed hard, tried to remember everything I had read, everything I had been told, and everything I had been doing for weeks in routine fashion. Giving it the throttle and lining the nose wheel up on the painted center stripe of the runway, I watched the airspeed gauge—25, 35, 45, 55, and then gently eased back on the yoke. There are few thrills to compare with the realization that you've done it—you're flying!

It took only a moment to realize that I still had to get this two-ton crate back safely on the ground. After a couple of circles around the field I decided to head in. Turning downwind, nose of the plane up, 115 knots, I began the check: fuel pump on, mixture rich, carb heat off, altitude 2000 and dropping. Turning on base, it was time to raise the nose, bank left, drift down to 800 feet, watch the altimeter and airspeed, and put the flaps down. Airspeed down to 105, flaps down one setting. Now don't let the nose of the plane pitch up. Now another flap setting, and now the instructor's words come back clear: "Always remember that at 55 knots, this crate is a *bird*... but at 54, she's a *rock!*" Don't let that airspeed fall too much!

On final, down to 600 feet, the trees begin to rush forward and upward, the threshold of the runway was racing toward me, and I remembered another of the instructor's sayings: "When you touch down, all the runway that's behind you is no good to you." So, touch down as close to this end of the runway as possible! Now close the throttle and glide on in ... nose up, nose up—the threshold flashes by, the plane seems to float for seconds, the airspeed warning buzzer begins to scream, then there is that blessed sound of tires smarting against concrete as we touch down.

Easy as pie. Then why am I sweating, and why is my instructor standing in a circle of cigarette butts?

Few thrills in my life can compare with that experience. I quit flying soon after I got my "ticket," because I felt the risk was too great. Perhaps not for others, but for me, since I did not fly that often, and because I realized that an airplane is mighty unforgiving of mistakes.

Meaningful Things in Life Carry a Risk

As I have pondered that experience, I realize it is a tremendous illustration of a basic truth: the most meaningful things in life carry a corresponding price tag of risk, of commitment, of cost.

If you are a young man, you will agree that it is much more fun to take the most beautiful girl in your class to the party than to take your sister! But the risk is greater. Will she even notice you, much less go with you? We would probably all agree that a big, thick, juicy steak fixed exactly as we like it is much better than a cold bologna sandwich. But the steak costs much more!

And this is true in the religious area of our lives as well. Consider the background of our text, Acts 13:13: "Now when Paul and his company loosed from Paphos, they came to Perga in Pamphylia: and John departing from them returned to Jerusalem."

Imagine the scene: Paul has announced to the church at Antioch that God has most surely called Barnabas, John Mark, and himself to missions. The church gathered for a great going-away reception in the "fellowship hall." The ladies all cried and hugged Paul, which made him uncomfortable, and the men solemnly shook hands all around, and then the trio took leave for Cyprus.

What a missionary trio that was—Paul, with his silver tongue and brilliant mind; Barnabas, the encourager, mature, and always there; John Mark, young and idealistic. They sailed to Cyprus where, in the words of an old hymn, they "like the whirlwind's breath, swept o'er all the earth." The governor of the island was converted, and great spiritual victories attended their work.

And then the trio sailed on to Asia Minor. And there a strange thing happened—John Mark turned back. Why? Scholars have proposed four major possibilities over the centuries: that he was fearful of the robbers on the dark roads of Asia Minor, that he was homesick, that a sweet young thing in Jerusalem beckoned, or that he was upset at the leadership role Paul increasingly took as the journey proceeded.

There is, however, another possibility. And that is, John Mark was responding to a basic concept in the Christian faith: *the call to risk.*

The Christian Life as Risk

The very nature of the Christian life is seen in the paradox of security and risk. Jesus said the person who wishes to save his life must be willing to lose it, and whoever loses his life for the sake of Christ and the gospel will surely save it.

The beginning of the Christian life is most certainly a call to risk. There is within each of us two spirits, and in the hour of conversion one of those spirits, the spirit of man, is saying to you, "You can run your own life! You don't want to be a weakling, a sissy, a Christian! Have some fun!" At the same time the other spirit, the Holy Spirit of God, is saying to you, "You were never meant to try to guide your own life! You will inevitably ruin your life—the only way to peace, joy, and fulfilment in your life is through inviting Jesus to be your Lord and Savior."

If you take Jesus as your Lord, you do so by making what we preachers often call the "leap of faith." You risk your future to the guidance of Jesus. It is said that the seventeenth-century French mathematician and philosopher, Blaise Pascal, formulated the "Great Wager." He put it this way: if I say there is *no* God, and then find at the end that there *is* such a God as the Bible teaches—then I've lost all. If I say there *is* such a God, and find at the end there is *no* such God, then I haven't lost anything; but if I say there *is* such a God, and find at the end that *He is,* then I have won all! He made the "Great Wager" and gave his heart to Christ. After Pascal's death a piece of paper was found sewn into the lining of his coat. The paper described his encounter with God, which radically changed the last decade of his life (he died at age thirty-nine). On the paper, dated November 23, 1654, were these words: "From about half past ten in the evening to about half an hour after midnight, Fire."

And the call to risk does not stop at conversion. We are still called upon to risk. Consider Abraham—he had already given up homeland and family to follow God into a land unknown, in a sort of conversion experience. Now, in Genesis 22, God calls on him to risk even more than we can easily imagine. "Give me your son!" To go to Mount Moriah and sacrifice Isaac would be to forfeit the future of the promise of God—for the blessing was to be through Isaac and his children. But to refuse to obey God was to forfeit the very ground of the promise—obedience to God. Yet that man would have killed his boy, had not God stayed his hand! The call to risk.

Or see Peter on the rooftop at Joppa, dozing, daydreaming, praying, in a trance, seeing the sheet full of unclean animals. God's command is in direct contradiction with all Peter has been taught as a good Jew, and all that he understands at that point as a Christian. But it becomes clear within minutes as Cornelius's messengers knock at the door below, desiring a preacher to come and share the gospel. Yet, by obeying God, Peter took a risk. He actually had to defend what he did in preaching to Gentiles before the church.

God calls us to a life of risk, growth, reaching out, both toward Him and for Him. Paul Tournier says having faith always means taking the risk implied in Pascal's wager—the risk of being unfaithful to God and being exposed by others; the risk of being beaten down by the devil and the world when we are trying to be faithful to God; the risk of being let down by other human beings when we seek to live out the life of grace; the risk of being laughed at by the world; the risk of losing our independence and being, truly, God's person.[2]

The Peace of Risk and the Risk of Peace

Perhaps you are feeling that the Christian life is too full of tension. "Preacher, I thought that being a Christian meant peace. After all, didn't Paul say the 'peace of God, which passeth all understanding' would guard our hearts?" Paul sure did, my brother, in the fourth chapter in Philippians, but in the preceding chapter he clearly wrote, "forgetting those things which are behind, and reaching forth unto those things which are before, I press toward the mark for the prize of the high calling of God . . ." (3:13-14).

There is a peace of God and a peace of godlessness. Let me describe that peace of godlessness. When I was a boy, I would sometimes get up early to go fishing in the cypress swamps. Before daylight we would get to the pond, quietly dip the water out of the old half-sunken boat, and begin to pole our way through the swamp. It was beautiful, and when the sun came up, stray rays of light filtered deep into the swamp, making a fairy circle on the water and lily pads. Poling quietly, all was still—save for a disturbed crane, slowly lumbering up from her nest and flapping off through the trees, or a little snake slithering away through the rushes. Finally, we reached the lake within the lake, an opening in the midst of the cypresses. How beautiful to behold, with the tall, gaunt cypress trees standing guard like sentinels, and the Spanish moss gently trembling in the dawn. A thin, velvety moss covered all the surface of that quiet glen. It was beautiful, and, oh, so peaceful—but it was dead! So it is with the peace of the godless. It may have its own appeal, but it is a dead peace.

There is another kind of peace that is alive and vibrant. Have you ever fished in mountain streams, and watched the water come dancing down the side of the mountain and through the high valleys—water that laughs, shouts, and bubbles as it weaves its way? It goes over, around, under the obstacles in its path, joyful all the time. And if you sit quietly at the edge of one of the pools where the water is clear at the surface, then boiling with foam and reflecting a glorious blue hue deeper down, you may be blessed by seeing the silver flash of a trout in the dark depths of the pool. This, too, is a kind of peace. But not a dead, stagnant peace. This is a peace that is alive and joyful and happy! That is the kind of peace to which God calls us—a faith that is on the move!

Maybe I can put the challenge of this sermon in one illustration—that of the circus. I love the circus, and some years ago when our children were small, I took them to see the Ringling Brothers circus. Well, matters were hectic for awhile as I made sure all of them had cokes, popcorn, hot dogs, and cotton candy. I didn't even mind bathrooming the kids during the part where the monkeys and bears come by riding the tricycles.

Finally came the interesting part. The action ceased in the two side rings, the floodlights were doused, the spotlight focused on Antonio Sylvester what's his name, standing at the base of the ladder leading up to the very pinnacle of the big top. As he climbed we all nervously talked about what a long fall that would be. I kept on eating popcorn and separating fighting children. At the top of the ladder he stood like a god, his shadow huge against the ceiling canvas. He dusted his hands with resin, checked the tape on his wrists, and began to swing the empty bar out into space. Soon another "daring young man on the flying trapeze" swung out from the other side; he was to be the "catcher" for our man. When the timing was right, a signal was given, and the drum roll began.

This is when I stopped eating popcorn, warned the kids, and stared up at the man on the little platform. For this is what I paid my money to see—the "daring young man" try for the magic "triple"; three somersaults in the air before being caught!

Sometimes they succeed; more often they don't.

I see John Mark doing that. With Paul and Barnabas he stands secure on the platform, basking in sure praise. But God called him to risk, to reach for the far bar, to go back to Jerusalem and undertake a task which will be misunderstood, even by Paul. But God's drum rolls, and the "daring young man" turns loose his grip on the certain, embraces risk, and tries for the far bar.

Does he make it? There pass silent decades before we know the answer. Then one day the old warrior Paul, in prison and ill, writes in a letter to friends these touching words: "Aristarchus my fellowprisoner saluteth you, and Marcus, sister's son to Barnabas, (touching whom ye received commandments: if he come unto you, receive him;)" And a little later he pens these pathetic words: "Only Luke is with me. Take Mark, and bring him with thee: for he is profitable to me for the ministry" (2 Tim. 4:11).

And then we turn to the earliest written account of the life of our Lord, the Gospel of Mark. And we find not the story of a gentle Jesus, meek and mild, but an account of the strong Son of God, who risked His life for us on the cross. And as we ponder all of this, we realize that Mark did not fail, nor did he turn tail and run from danger. Rather, he answered a call of God to risk, to go for the far bar, and he made it!

But we are not concerned with John Mark so much as with your own relationship to God. For God calls *you* to risk, to abandon Adam's way, to give your heart to Christ. He calls on you to risk all you are, and ever will be, to Christ. Will you do it?

9
The Diary of a Lonely Woman
John 4:7-30,39-42

The woman saith unto him, Sir, give me this water, that I thirst not, neither come hither to draw (John 4:15).

These haunting words gather up the deep need of the woman at the well. The account of Jesus' meeting the woman at the well in John 4 is one of the most vivid stories of the New Testament. Notice the word pictures in the account.

"He must needs go through Samaria" (v. 4). The Greek text reveals a determination, a steadfast resolution on the part of the Master before which men fell back in amazement. The trek through Samaria, which no Jew was overly fond of making, took Jesus by the city of Sychar in Samaria.

"Now Jacob's well was there. Jesus therefore, being wearied with his journey, sat thus on the well: and it was about the sixth hour" (v. 6). Here is the weary Christ, the human Christ which we need to see. Further on in the story, Jesus speaks with the woman who comes to draw water at the well while the disciples are in the city buying food. She then says to Him, "Sir, thou hast nothing to draw with, and the well is deep" (v. 11). Christ without a bucket! And toward the close of the story the woman is so excited over what Jesus knows and says about her that she leaves her pot on the edge of the well and runs back into the city!

All these factors are the marks of an eyewitness account. Here we are shown treasures from the heart and memory of this woman at the well. Is it possible that she kept a diary? These vivid and personal touches in this story have the earmarks of a page torn from the diary of a lonely, confused, and sinful housewife.

There many ways to look at this woman: sinful, adulterous, saucy, flirtatious, lonely, hurting. I think the word *lonely* would appear often in her diary. I know this woman well—I have met her in every church I have pastored, I have seen her in every revival meeting I have ever preached.

In fact, I think I met this woman when I was a child. She lived right behind the house in which I grew up, so from our backyard we children could look over the fence at her modest green stucco home. We knew—oh, did we know!—exactly where she received the money for the Buick automobile which was parked in the yard. Oh, yes, the man who owned the liquor store down the street claimed her as his girl. We kids used to stare at her whenever we would see her in the yard, and then we would run back to our house. She was an evil woman . . . or so all the churchgoing people said. But, you know, I don't remember seeing even one church person visit that home. And in these thirty-five years since, I have wondered why somebody didn't invite her to church.

The First Word in Her Diary Is: Lonely

There are many kinds of loneliness. There is the loneliness Abraham must have felt, as he pulled up roots and went off into a strange land at the mysterious and hard-to-put-your-finger-on guidance of the Lord. There is the loneliness of Rizpah, the wife of Saul, as she flapped her rags in the wind to scare the buzzards away from the hanging corpses of her seven sons. There is the loneliness of Hosea, cast aside by a wanton wife. There is the loneliness which Jesus experienced in the Garden of Gethsemane as He prepared to go to the cross for you and me.

But the kind of loneliness which gripped the heart of the woman at the well was first experienced by Eve in the Garden of Eden. It is a kind of loneliness which is the direct result of disobedience to God, the loneliness which comes from rebelling from God and telling Him to mind His own business; then finding that you cannot run your own life. No trucker plans to have to use the "runaway truck" lanes on mountain roads, but they are there because trucks run away regardless of the intentions of the driver. So it is with our lives; we think we can manage them, and the loneliness of the woman at the well is one result.

Her sinfulness in her own eyes and in the eyes of men made her an outcast and added to her loneliness. She could feel the judgmental eyes of every woman in the village as she shopped. She had to run the gauntlet of the village street for every jug of water she drank. That is why she came to the well at high noon instead of with the other women in the cool of the evening. That is why she came alone.

Her loneliness carried a sharp edge—she had a sauciness, a kind of cattiness. She was good at cutting other people down. We can see that side of her personality as she jests with Jesus, putting on a futile mask, playing the part of the religious woman.

When Jesus asks her for a drink of water, notice that she has no hesitation about striking up a conversation and, indeed, seeking to belittle Christ. In modern vernacular, she says something like: "Well, that's a new one! A Jew who'll stoop to ask a cup of water from a Samaritan woman!" To Jesus' response that if she knew who He really was, she would be asking a drink from Him, she replies in mock seriousness that the well was deep—I can see her bending to look over into the well and shaking her head in mock despair —and he has no rope nor bucket! As Jesus assures her that anyone drinking of the water He could give would never thirst again, she jokingly asks for that water so she would no longer have to draw at the well.

Suddenly Jesus brought her to her senses. "Go, call thy husband, and come hither" (v. 16). And pain, like a knife, cut her heart. See her flush as she responds haughtily: "I have no husband" (v. 17). And the Master of all hearts gently told her, "Thou hast well said, I have no husband: For thou hast had five husbands; and he whom thou now hast is not thy husband" (vv. 17-18).

The Second Word in the Diary of a Lonely Woman: Guilt

As Jesus sat by the well watching His disciples dwindle away in the distance, perhaps He began to study the woman approaching with her burden of the water jug. But the Master knew the jar was not the biggest burden she bore The guilt feelings she carried were much heavier.

As a high schooler I wondered if Nathaniel Hawthorne had not overdone his emphasis on guilt in *The Scarlet Letter*. The deep burden of guilt ruined both the young minister, Arthur Dimmesdale, and his partner in sin, Hester Prynne. And the entire book is a study in the effects of guilt—psychological, physical, and emotional. I now know, as a physician of souls, that Hawthorne has not at all overstated his case.

Our worship services are broadcast in the Mid-south over both television and radio, and our media congregation is encouraged to phone in their prayer requests. Typical of such requests are the following, with names changed:

> Ruth: "I need a good job, I need this man out of my life. I'm tired of the life I'm living—I want a new life!"
>
> Jane: "I have been divorced for two years, and have not been in church since. My mother died about a year ago. I'm twenty-one years old, and there is a great vacuum in my life."
>
> Concerning Susan, our telephone counselor wrote: "She says she went to church last Sunday for the first time in a long while. Her prayer request is that she may overcome sin in her life."
>
> About Donna, the counselor wrote: "She is coming up on marijuana charges Monday morning. Now on probation, she will probably be in jail for about a year. She has a two-year-old son. Says she is a Christian, has been saved. Ashamed to continually ask Jesus for forgiveness. Please pray for her.

People are no different now than when Jesus walked on this earth. We have a common kinship with this woman at the well, as she puts on her mask, picks up her water jug, and prepares for her walk to the well. Within is a dark swamp of guilt, depressing her and robbing her of all feelings of worth.

She tries to belittle Jesus, mock His comments concerning spiritual things, and finally hurries on to talk of religion when she perceives He is a religious teacher. We have religion in our bones if not on our lips. Raised in the synagogue, she was. Can you hear the wistful tone of her voice as she declares, "I know that Messiah cometh, which is called Christ: when he is come, he will tell us all things" (v. 25). When the Messiah comes, all will be different!

The rest of the conversation is left to our imagination as the writer indicates the disciples now have returned. The woman hurries away—leaving us a third word with which to describe her.

The Third Word in The Diary of a Lonely Woman: Understood

"Come, see a man, which told me all things that ever I did: is not this the Christ?" (v. 29). Here is a man who knows all about her, yet understands her. He does not reject her, He does not condemn her—could this be the Christ? On the way into the village and as she comes back with a crowd, she is putting the gospel together.

She realizes that *God knows us better than we know ourselves.* God knows all about us:

> Like as a father pitieth his children, so the Lord pitieth them that fear him. For he knoweth our frame; he remembereth that we are dust. He hath not dealt with us after our sins; nor rewarded us according to our iniquities. For as the heaven is high above the earth, so great is his mercy toward them that fear him (Ps. 103:13-14, 10-11).

She is beginning to *experience reconciliation*—to know the forgiveness of God, to find the strange power of a love that will not let us go, and to know the new sense of being clean within. "Come, see a man which told me all that ever

I did." A man who does not judge, but understands, and forgives.

The real problem of modern lonely housewives, doctors, lawyers, merchants, or chiefs is not the terrible secret about what they've been, but the unrealized secret of what their lives (and ours) can be! The city shunned her because she knew too much—about life, about sin, about their men. Only Jesus pitied her for what she did not know: "If you knewest the gift of God, and who it is that saith to thee, Give me to drink" (v. 10).

The Fourth Word in the Diary of a Lonely Woman: Witness

The final scene of this story is the village coming out to see "the man which told me all that ever I did." In verse 42 there is a strange comment: "Now we believe, not because of thy saying: for we have heard him ourselves, and know that this is indeed the Christ, the Saviour of the world." We all believed at first because someone else told us of the living water—then we met Jesus and discovered for ourselves that He will do for our loneliness, guilt, and misunderstanding what He has done for others.

Some years ago in a sermon I shared the gist of a letter from a young lady who had crippled her life with her sin and rebellion. A few days later I received the following letter from a different girl:

> Dear Dr. Davis,
>
> After hearing your sermon yesterday, I feel compelled to write you concerning the girl who went off to college and moved

in with her boyfriend. I sat fighting back tears as I listened, for until some months ago, her story was mine.

Only someone who's been where she is can understand it. That's why I'm sending you a letter to her. I hope there's some way you can get it to her. I'm not signing my name.

There were times back when I considered coming to you myself, but I didn't want to put my name or my face with that story. God and I alone got me through it, but it was almost too hard.

Anyway, use your best judgment on sending her my letter. I will try to call sometime and see if she got it.

Sincerely,

A Friend

That note to me, and the fourteen-page letter to the first girl is sad but eloquent testimony to the fact that the woman at the well is legion. And the tragic part is that so many of us drift on without meeting Christ. As I write this, there is lying on my desk the letter I forwarded to the first girl. It came back, unopened, stamped with this notice: *Return to sender. Moved—left no address.* Whoever you are, wherever you are, whatever your past—Jesus will help you.

10
Pretonius
(A Monologue Sermon)

And when the centurion, which stood over against him, saw that he so cried out, and gave up the ghost, he said, Truly this man was the son of God (Mark 15:39).

My name is Pretonius—some of you know me as Longinus. In my old age you think of me only as a Christian leader, your bishop. Some of you, knowing my past sufferings and imprisonments for the gospel, wonder how long it will be before my faith will get me into more serious trouble, perhaps costing me my life.

You are right—the storm clouds are gathering, and this may be the last time I can speak to you, my beloved friends and fellow followers of our Lord Jesus Christ, to whom be glory and praise forever. Amen! I must hasten to speak to you as a dying man to dying men, for some of you will surely drink of the same cup I will soon be offered.

I want to tell you about the one day I spent in the presence of our Lord. It seems so long ago, and not many still remain with us who had such an experience. Our brother Peter has departed from us to be with the Lord, and we are all still shocked to hear that Paul was beheaded at Rome. Nevertheless, I too had the wonderful privilege to be close to Jesus one entire day.

Before I tell you of my day with our Master, let me ask

you a question: If you could have such a glorious opportunity as spending a day with Jesus in his ministry as I did, what day would you choose? Through the years I have asked fellow Christians that, and received many different answers. Some would choose a day in the youth of Jesus, working beside him in the carpenter shop. Others would like to have been with him that day as he walked by the shore of the Sea of Galilee and called Peter to follow him. Some would cherish the idea of being with him when he healed the sick at Capernaum, maybe that day when the man was let down through the roof—Peter's roof—because the crowd was so great they couldn't get in the front door.

Or maybe you'd choose that day at Caesarea Philippi when Jesus asked the twelve, "Who do you think I am?" I've often thought, myself, how wonderful it would have been to have heard the sermon He preached on the mountainside. I can just see the people all seated in groups, looking from a distance like a giant flower bed in their bright colored robes, ah, well. My day with the Master was so different, yet so full of meaning.

I was a young man then—nearly forty years ago. I ought to tell you I came from a poor Roman family without any political standing. I joined the army and gradually moved up in the ranks until I became a noncommissioned officer, a centurion, commanding 100 soldiers.

My life was fairly obscure and uneventful, too, until I was stationed in Judea. I was on duty at Fortress Antonia, just north of where the great Temple stood until recently. It was in the feast days of Passover, and one day word came from the procurator, Pontius Pilate, to go and arrest a certain troublemaker. I detailed a cohort—fifty of my men—

and started out for the rendezvous. There wasn't anything striking about the order because the city was full of rabble-rousers and the atmosphere was always volatile at feast times.

I do remember that even then I didn't like the smell of it—the man's "friend" was to betray Him to us. When we reached the garden where we were to arrest Him, I well remember how calm He was—although all His friends took to their heels. The calmness was like something shining out from Jesus' face. There was a slight tone of hurt in His voice as He turned to me and simply said: "Why have you come out here like a posse after a common thief? I have been teaching in the Temple every day; you could have taken me anytime." It was only then that I remembered how I had seen Him; I had watched the scenes unfold in the Temple court from the windows of the fortress. Several times in the last few days I had seen Him.

We bound Him, and then took Him to that shell of an old man, Annas. He was the father-in-law to Caiaphas, the high priest. Then we trudged on over to Caiaphas's house. By this time it was midnight; but you'd have thought it was midday with all the lights and people there. The Sanhedrin had been called together, and there was enough rule-keeping, pride, ego, and starched faces in that one house that night to run the whole city on for a week! I delivered my prisoner as Pilate had told me to, and then stood back to watch the situation. Pilate hated these Pharisees' guts, yet he had to get along with them, so I was to take the prisoner to them and hope they would take things from there.

It was a mockery. What was supposed, by their law, to be a trial was really a badly bungled frame-up. Apparently two or three "expert" witnesses failed to show. Those who were hastily impressed to testify could not agree on the crime the man had done—there were jumbled efforts to accuse Him of claiming to be God; of planning to tear down the Temple and build it back single-handedly in three days; and things like that.

Finally, when things were hopelessly bogged down and the efforts to discredit Jesus were becoming an embarrassing mess, Caiaphas himself decided to get right into the middle of it. "I command you," he said, "to tell us whether you are the Christ, the Son of God." Jesus' answer was soft and direct, and carried all over the room: "That's what you are saying. And I tell you, that one day you will see the Son of man sitting on the right hand of power, and coming in the clouds of heaven."

That did it. Caiaphas tore his robes—not a big tear, mind you—as a symbol that Jesus had committed blasphemy. To me, a Roman soldier, it was a curious custom which I had never seen before. Instantly, the whole place turned into a madhouse. Pandemonium reigned. They all began to tear their robes—carefully. The older men wailed and held their heads, while the younger men, to prove their manhood and godliness, proceeded to spit on Jesus and slap Him. What they knew was that we Romans were charged to keep the prisoner under control in such circumstances; what they didn't know was that Jesus would not even try to strike them back. Some of them mocked Him and beat Him over the head. I quickly saw that things were out of hand, and waded into the fray with my men and got things back under control.

It was moving on well past midnight, and we were told to guard the prisoner until sunup and bring Him again before this august body at their quarters in the Temple portico. I did it, though it meant the entire night was shot. My men were in no mood for foolishness when we met with the Sanhedrin again at dawn. It was a shorter meeting, called simply because the Sanhedrin had some rule against meeting at night, and therefore they must meet in daylight to pronounce sentence on Jesus. They found Him guilty of blasphemy and deserving of death. I, even at that point, found him guilty of nothing more than being different from them!

We then dragged Him off to Pilate, where they would request the Roman government to do the dirty work. The Jews no longer had the power in their religious courts to carry out a death sentence.

Pilate was at the old royal palace of Herod, where he stayed when he came down from Caesarea for the religious feasts. We waited in the courtyard, and finally Pilate appeared at the podium, sleepy, disgusted, and angry. You could have cut the tension with a knife; but it was always that way. The Jews hated Pilate, and it was mutual. The Jews wouldn't go in—they would be defiled!

"Are you a king?" Pilate decided he might as well have some entertainment, or maybe he was half-serious. Jesus' answers gave him little satisfaction—"My kingdom is not of this world." "I came to bear witness of the truth." Again Pilate probed, "What is the truth?"

Tiring of this situation, Pilate announced that he found nothing in this man worthy of death. The mob spirit began to build, and the leaders were screaming how Jesus inflamed people from Galilee to Jerusalem! Pilate picked up on Galilee, and when they said Jesus was from Nazareth, Pilate told us to take Him to King Herod Antipas, who was in town.

Jesus spoke not a word to that old fox, Herod. That one soon grew bored of such a prisoner and suggested my soldiers clothe Him in an old royal robe, and have sport with Him. They did, slapping Him around, crushing a "crown" of thorns down upon His head, and generally acting like fools until I had enough and took him back to Pilate.

Give Pilate credit. He tried. He took Jesus inside and talked, then came back and did his best to save the man. I had to stay with the prisoner, so I went inside with Jesus. "Why not just whip the man?" The Jews weren't happy with Pilate's effort, but he had Jesus whipped anyhow. It was while they were scourging him that Pilate's wife slipped a note to Pilate, which he read out loud: "Don't have anything to do with this man Jesus—I had a terrible dream about him last night."

When Jesus was returned, I thought surely this would satisfy even the Sanhedrin. Have you ever seen Roman soldiers scourge a Jew? Probably not. They tie the man to a post, bare his back, and beat him with a long whip made of several leather thongs, and at the tip of each thong is a piece of metal or bone, or something sharp. Men often die in the midst of such a beating. When they brought Jesus back, Pilate winced at the sight, and then made that statement which all we Christians spend our lives saying: *Ecce Homo!*—Behold the Man!

The crowd did—and roared for His execution! Nothing Pilate suggested would pacify them—whipping, releasing Him as the traditional freed prisoner at the feast—why, they actually begged for a murderer to be set free!

I stood there disgusted with both Pilate and the crowd as he ordered a silver wash basin be brought. Then he elaborately washed his hands and screamed at the mob—"See to it; my hands are clean! His blood be on you!" And over and over they chanted: "His blood on us—and our children! His blood on us—and our children!"

And so the order was given for my men and me to carry out the sentence of death by crucifixion upon Jesus of Nazareth.

I went first, on horseback, clearing a path. Behind me came a legionnaire holding high the red-and-white Roman standard with its eagle on top. Next came the prisoner—or rather, the three prisoners, for since we were executing Jesus, Pilate reasoned that two others awaiting execution might be taken care of as well. Each man carried the crossbeam of his cross, staggering, slipping, plodding. Behind the prisoners came the soldiers, six to a rank, spears on shoulders; the might of Rome to kill three men! Last in the procession were the members of the Sanhedrin, and then the mob closed in behind, filling the streets with people.

At the city gate the Sanhedrin kicked their mules to a canter, and headed up to the hill to get a good seat. It wasn't far. There it loomed—not a high hill as hills go, but high enough and close enough to the main road leading north out of Jerusalem to make Him a spectacle as He died.

But we weren't there yet, and He stumbled on the dusty path. I wasn't surprised; as I say, men often die under the whip before they get to the hill. I wheeled and ordered a man—he stood out because he was a black man—"You there; yes, you—shoulder that crossbeam and make yourself useful!" I had no way of knowing that that man, Simon of Cyrene, would become my brother through the blood shed on that hill that day. You know his sons, Alexander and Rufus, both leaders in this church.

I watched Him die. You see me wearing no cross as some of you. For me it was an instrument of death, degradation, punishment, disgrace, and defeat. For me it is the most repulsive thing in the world. We didn't just kill them; we amused ourselves with their pain; it was brutal torture.

I have seen prisoners shrieking as if they were mad as we approached the place of execution. They have groveled at my feet, whining for mercy. I have watched them struggle with the soldiers, fighting futilely to escape. They bite, curse, jerk—sometimes it took six men to hold a man down while the nails were driven.

But from this man there was no sound. There was a great silence at His cross. The quiet weeping of the women, the silent circling of the vultures, the screaming of the thieves on either side, the grunting of the soldiers at their work—all of us who have ever done such a thing are haunted forever by the sound of hammer on nail.

We bound the arms of the men to the crossbeams to support them, and hauled the crossbeam up to the top of the upright with ropes.

Then we waited. Watched. Listened. It was happening to me then, I realize, as I think back on it. I saw civilized men, religious leaders, become animals—spitting, jeering, laughing at these poor men who were as good as dead! "He saved others—let him now save himself!" "If thou be the king of Israel, come down." And those folks passing by joined in the grim fun. It was hideous.

My men sat down to while away the time. They divided up the belongings of the dying men—all except His seamless robe, which they gambled for, putting sticks in a helmet and drawing for the robe. Then they lay down in the noonday heat to eat their bread and cheese and drink wine and doze.

As long as I live, I will never forget the contrast. He was an island of faith, courage, and love in the midst of a sea of hate.

His words are as clear as if it were yesterday. He looked at me and said: "Father, forgive them, for they know not what they do" (Luke 23:34). I remember thinking, suppose there is only *one* God, not Mars, Jupiter, and the rest, but one true God, this man's father!

He then spoke to a woman, His mother. Had I known it was His mother, I would have kept her away from that place.

Out of the heavy darkness that cloaked the city from noon until three in the afternoon, He spoke—and I shall never forget the eerie sound of His words: "Eli, Eli, lama sabachthani!"—My God, my God, why have you left me? (Matt 27:46).

And finally he said, "Father, into thy hands I commend my spirit!" (Luke 23:46). It was a shout of victory!

I remember how depressed the whole thing made me—it was not an ordinary crucifixion. Then the darkness at noon. And the earthquake when He bowed His head and died. I felt compelled by I don't know what—to take off my helmet. Then I knelt down, and what I said then I say now and ever shall say to all men: "This man was the Son of God" (Matt. 15:39).

Nothing was the same as I stood up. The sky was not as dark; the crowd was beginning to leave, satisfied now; the man sagged on the cross. I barked the clean-up orders—to break the legs of the men who were not yet dead. I went back to the barracks, not really sure of who I was—although I was more and more sure of who He was!

A summons came from Pilate, who wanted to know if the man who called himself king was dead. "Yes, he's dead!" But somehow I didn't fully believe that.

Next day I was summoned again by Pilate. "Pretonius, hear these men. They want a guard; they say the man Jesus prophesied He would rise from the dead." Then, to the Jews standing there looking uncomfortable at the very idea, he said, "Pretonius and his men are yours. Set a guard at the grave—and make it as sure as you can!"

I didn't personally go to the grave, but my men said there was a blinding flash just at dawn on the second morning they guarded, and the tomb was open and empty when they recovered their sight. I was troubled; I couldn't sleep. I now know God was in the desire of the lady Procla, Pilate's wife, to journey to Galilee to see if the rumors were really true that the Galilean were indeed alive. I was assigned to accompany her, and there I met Him again—alive forevermore!

That was my day with the Master. I have met Him many times since, and I tell about Him to all who will listen to my story. I feel an urge from above to ask you, my friends who have gathered here in this catacomb for this service— Have you met Him?

> When I survey the wondrous cross,
> On which the Prince of glory died,
> My richest gain I count but loss,
> And pour contempt on all my pride.

Were the whole realm of nature mine,
That were a present far too small;
Love so amazing, so divine,
Demands my soul, my life, my all.

—Isaac Watts

11
Why Is the Devil So Mad?
Matthew 12:22-29; Revelation 12

Or else how can one enter into a strong man's house, and spoil his goods, except he first bind the strong man? and then he will spoil his house (Matt. 12:29).

Popular programs of Bible prophecy focus in on the winding down of this old world. The last days, the signs of the times, an eschatalogical road map—whatever title we give our thoughts about the end, we all include a common element: *the devil.*

All the major elements of Bible prophecy are related to the person and activity of the devil. For instance, to speak of the signs of the last days is to talk of a growing struggle with the devil and the evil he masterminds. The search—tantalizing but ill-founded biblically—for an Anti-christ in the future is a search for the great representative of the devil in the last days. The doctrine of the rapture of the church has many aspects, not the least of which is: it is the escape of the church from the power and presence of the devil. Whatever view of the tribulation of the end times one holds, it is a time of the unleashing of the full fury and poisonous rage of the devil on the earth. The battle of Armageddon is that great climactic battle in which the legions of the devil are to be defeated, and the binding of Satan is necessary to allow the millennium, the one thousand years of peace upon the earth.

Realizing that the devil is a reality and does figure prominently in these last days, I want us to look at another aspect of the devil—his anger. His anger at the church, at you, and at me.

Turn in your Bible to Revelation 12. This chapter is one of the most important chapters of this often-misunderstood book. In this chapter we have a beautiful and fearful interpretation of the Christmas story, but that is another sermon. My aim right now is for us to see how the writer gives his interpretation of the battle between the church and the devil in such a way as to strengthen, comfort, and encourage the early Christians.

The first scene in this chapter is that of the *beautiful woman,* clothed with the sun and using the moon for her footstool. She wears a crown of twelve stars, and is about to bring forth a child (vs. 1-2). This is a picture of Old Testament Israel, God's chosen people from whom should come, in the flesh, the Messiah.

The second scene (vs. 3-4) is dominated by a *great red dragon,* so huge and hideous that the sweep of his tail drags down a third of the stars of heaven. He stands before the woman, waiting to devour the child as soon as it is born.

In verse 5, *the child is born*—a man child, the Messiah. And squeezed into this one verse we see the whole ministry, death, resurrection, and ascension of our Lord. The writer's majestic sweep of Jesus down into history and back up again into the heavenly realm leads us to remember the touching passage Paul pens in Philippians 2 about Jesus laying aside His glory to come to earth to take up the form, life, and death of a servant—and then to receive the homage of every tongue and every knee.

The next scene picturing the *great war in heaven* (vs. 7-9) is subject to various interpretations. It is safe to say that John felt the birth of this child Jesus created a tremendous upset in the spiritual forces of this universe. The devil lost some sort of standing, power, and grip he had on this old world in the birth, life, death, and resurrection of that babe.

I would emphasize one other scene in this chapter, the *effort of the devil to destroy the woman* (vs. 13-17). The woman is no longer Old Testament Israel who gives birth to the Messiah. She is now the New Testament church, created by the Messiah! Now notice verse 17: "And the dragon was wroth with the woman, and went to make war with the remnant of her seed, which do keep the commandments of God, and have the testimony of Jesus Christ."

Here is a terrifying statement. It may be that you have never had your attention drawn to this verse and its implications for your life. The devil is mad at every Christian, and that includes *you* if you are a follower of Christ! Little old you! Why is the devil mad at you? Take your pencil and let's discover three reasons why the devil is so mad at you, and write them in the margin of your Bible.

Because He Realizes These Are the Last Days

The very phrase "the last days" sets off all kinds of bells, depending on what approach to eschatology you grew up with, or have been accustomed to hearing. The biblical idea of the "last days" has nothing to do with calendar time. It is more the idea of a certain kind of time, a quality of days.

We have been living in the "last days" since the ministry of Jesus.

In Acts 2:14-21, Peter stood up on the day of Pentecost to defend, as he thought, the other apostles who were being accused of drunkenness. Instead, God spoke powerfully through him that day for conviction of lost souls. But notice that Peter quoted the Old Testament prophet Joel, who said certain things would happen in the "last days":

> But this is that which was spoken by the prophet Joel; And it shall come to pass in the last days, saith God, I will pour out of my Spirit upon all flesh: and your sons and your daughters shall prophesy, and your young men shall see visions, and your old men shall dream dreams (vv. 16-17).

That, says Peter, is *this*! The last days had come and have continued for twenty centuries! In 1 John 2:18 the writer declared it was the last hour, and that anti-christs were already among the Christians.

So, then, when we speak of the "last days" in the biblical sense, we don't mean there are only a few more calendar days or months or years before the end of the world. That may be the case, but the term "last days" means that ever since Jesus came, every day has a certain kind of flavor—the flavor of an impending judgment and a shortness of time, a flavor of victory, a flavor of completion of all that is necessary for redemption, and a flavor of the defeat of Satan!

That cry on the cross, "It is finished!" has cast a glow over the church for two thousand years and warmed the hearts of those who love Jesus, for He stands at the door, whether it be a day or a thousand years before He ends this world.

For these twenty centuries the devil has known that he is doomed—and that fact is largely responsible for his great wrath. Listen to the latter part of verse 12 of Revelation 12: "For the devil is come down unto you, having great wrath, because he knoweth that he hath but a short time."

He knows his time is short, and with that dark knowledge in his heart he stalks the earth as a roaring lion, seeking whom he may devour. It is a sobering thought to realize that the devil knows the Book of Revelation better than any preacher here on earth. He knows how things are going to work out! He is a cornered dog with no escape.

To see how the devil thinks in these last days, remember Hitler. It was all over for him in the summer of 1942 when Rommel and his Afrika Corps were defeated at El Alamein. But with his crazed mind, Hitler kept fighting harder, more furiously, sacrificing his armies without any reservations, and then cowering in his Berlin bunker for the end. Just so the devil knows he has no appeal to a higher court; when this world comes to an end, that is his end, too. This fact must be like a pounding drum in his fevered brain.

A clue to understanding the crazed thinking of the devil is seen in Matthew 8:29. Jesus had crossed over to the country of the Gadarenes when He was met by two men possessed with devils; men who lived in the nearby tombs and were so fierce they scared people away. As Matthew tells it: "And, behold, they cried out, saying, What have we to do with thee, Jesus, thou Son of God? Art thou come hither to torment us before the time?"

No matter how much time is left—it is not enough for the devil! And this is why he is so devious, so dangerous. He must pedal harder, he must "make hay while the sun shines."

So mark it down and remember it well, Christian—the devil hates you because you are his enemy, and his time for defeating you is short! Like Martin Luther, we had better throw the ink well at him and recognize his power and his ultimate defeat. Luther no doubt had the devil in mind as he penned these lines:

> And tho this world, with devils filled,
> Should threaten to undo us,
> We will not fear, for God hath willed
> His truth to triumph thro' us.
> The Prince of Darkness grim,
> We tremble not for him;
> His rage we can endure,
> For lo! his doom is sure:
> One little word shall fell him.

Mark it down and remember it well, you who are not Christians—the devil wants your soul more than you can imagine, for he wants you as part of his already doomed rebellion against God. He wants you to experience his eternal agony, anxiety, and separation from God Almighty.

Because He Is Already Crippled

Is the devil really crippled? As Henry Martin, our assistant pastor here at First Baptist Church, Memphis, commented in my preparation of this sermon: The devil sure is getting around on that one leg! Is the devil really crippled? The Bible says he is. And this is a second reason for his fury.

Turn in your Bible to Matthew 12 and we will mark

down the proof for the crippled state of Satan in these days—and that makes him furious at you! Let me give you the setting of verses 22 through 29. Jesus was healing people and casting out demons with such power that people were saying, "Is not this the Son of David?" (v. 23). But the Pharisees were saying, "This fellow doth not cast out devils, but by Beelzebub the prince of the devils" (v. 24). In other words, the Pharisees were accusing Jesus of being in cahoots with the devil!

Jesus pointed out how foolish it was to accuse Him of supporting the Devil, when He fought the devil at every turn. In verses 27 through 29, we have the beginning of the idea of the binding of Satan:

> And if I by Beelzebub cast out devils, by whom do your children cast them out? therefore they shall be your judges. But if I cast out devils by the Spirit of God, then the kingdom of God is come unto you. Or else how can one enter into a strong man's house, and spoil his goods, except he first bind the strong man? and then he will spoil his house.

Jesus is making several points here that we need to understand and mark down. First, He is saying that this world is *under the dominion of Satan.* This world and its inhabitants are the "house" of Satan. Maybe we don't like to realize that, but, after all, possession is nine-tenths of the law! The "goods" of the devil's house are the souls of men—your soul, my soul. Jesus is also saying that He has invaded the devil's territory, broken into his house! What a powerful way to describe what was accomplished in the life, death, and resurrection of Jesus. But notice also that Jesus said one could not break into the house of a strong man and steal his goods unless the strong man were *first bound.* He was declaring that in His ministry Satan was being bound.

Now I firmly believe this passage, which has its parallels in Mark 3:20-30 and Luke 11:14-23, is the basis for the "binding" symbolism in Revelation 20. While none of us can speak on such things with certainty, I feel the biblical meaning of the "binding" passage, and its power for our time, is best seen in the light of the fact that Jesus bound Satan in His own ministry. I believe that the "thousand years" of Satan's binding began in the ministry of Jesus and will continue until Jesus returns to earth.

All of this means that Satan is bound and crippled, even now. We cannot imagine his fury if he were not bound! What is meant by the "binding" of Satan? How is he crippled? *Satan is bound with reference to his power in the life of the Christian.* The presence of the Holy Spirit in the believer's life effectively cripples the power and influence of Satan in that particular life. This crippling of the devil's power is not effective in the lives of those who do not belong to Christ. The full power of the devil is unleashed on the non-Christian, even though he may not be aware of it, for by this same passage we understand that these people already belong to Satan. And to take them away from him is like trying to take a bone away from a dog!

So mark it down, Christian, the devil *is* bound in these days, and that has doubled his anger at you, for your Lord bound this prince of darkness. Mark it down, you who are yet in the dominion and rule of Satan. He is crippled and will have no mercy on you.

Because He Has Failed to Destroy the Church of Jesus Christ

There is the sound of trumpets in this third reason for Satan's anger. Indeed, the church of Jesus, made up of those who have been redeemed in the great raid upon the devil's dominion, is not cringing! Jesus declared that His church would be as a mighty army with banners waving, charging the very gates of hell itself! Notice the marks of the church as found in Revelation 12:11-17. The church is described as the people who keep the commandments of God and have the testimony of Jesus Christ. They *keep the commandments.* Some things are clear and certain, black and white. The church is committed to God and His will. The church has the *testimony.* The writer has in mind more than a five-minute prayer-meeting testimony by one who has long since become too old to be tempted by the sins he proclaims victory over! They have the reality of Jesus' presence and others sense it.

The life of Andrew Murray is an outstanding example of what it means to have the presence of Christ, and to have His presence in such a manner that others sense it. Murray was a pastor in Wellington, South Africa, during the nineteenth century. After his death at age eighty-nine, his friends erected a beautiful marble statue of him with the face toward the street. "So great is the esteem felt for him that drunken people staggering to their wretched hovels fear to pass that way home, for, they said, 'The old minister will see us.' Even when intoxicated and incapable, they tremble to pass by so much as his likeness in stone, so holy had been his life among them."[1]

They are not afraid for their Christianity to cost them

something. At a recent Baptist World Alliance meeting in Berlin I heard Billy Kim, the notable evangelist of Korea, tell of a young girl's testimony in that troubled land a few years ago. Communist troops had rounded up the Christians of a village, marched the group to a church, and there proceeded to demand they forfeit either their faith or their lives. A large picture of Jesus was placed on the floor and the Christians were commanded to pass by the picture, one by one, spitting on it as an act of renunciation of their faith.

The first man spat on the picture and moved to the other side of the church. After a pause, the second man did likewise, and a third and fourth. Then came a teenage girl to the picture. She stood for a moment, then knelt and wiped the spittle off the picture, and kissed it. "I cannot renounce Jesus—go ahead and shoot me," she called softly. The soldiers hesitated, unsure what to do in such a situation, then angrily dismissed the crowd because of the uproar caused by the girl's witness. As they left, the crowd heard four shots. Later it was noised about that the Communists shot those who renounced their faith—they were not fit to be Communists!

The devil has failed to destroy the church as the body of Christ, the institution of God on earth. The devil has failed to destroy you as an individual Christian. Pause and think with me about how God in His infinite mercy has preserved you in trials and tribulations, and given you the power to overcome, even as the saints of the first century.

The church is secure. You and I as Christians are safe. The devil is doomed, but furious in his death throes. Let us plead with our families, our friends, our acquaintances to come to the protection of the blood of Christ, our Savior.

12
Abraham: No Easy Faith
Genesis 22:3-10

After these things the word of the Lord came unto Abram in a vision, saying, Fear not, Abram: I am thy shield, and thy exceeding great reward (Gen. 15:1).

Abraham is one of the most fascinating men in the entire Bible. He is claimed by three world religions: Judaism, Christianity, and Islam. His name appears 188 times in the Koran, the sacred book of the Muslims. The apostle Paul uses him as the model of faith in his letter to the Romans (See Rom. 4:2-3,5) Jesus spoke highly of Abraham, saying that they shall come from the north, east, south, and west and sit down in the kingdom of God with Abraham (See Luke 13:29). In Luke 16, in the parable of the rich man and Lazarus, heaven is depicted by Lazarus being "in the bosom of Abraham" (vv. 22-23, author). Jesus once declared, "Abraham rejoiced to see my day" (John 8:56). And three times in the Holy Scriptures Abraham is called the "friend of God." One man—and only one—in the New Testament is paid the high honor of Jesus calling him a "son of Abraham."

Wouldn't you like to have the kind of spiritual stature Abraham had? What is his secret? What made him the kind of man that three world religions want to claim him as their spiritual father?

His secret is the same which immortalized the running of Eric Liddell. In the 1924 Olympics, the "Flying Scotsman," a twenty-two-year-old science student from Edinburgh University, won a gold medal in the 400-meter race. Of course, there were others who won gold medals at those games, among them Johnny Weissmuller, who went on to become "Tarzan."

But Eric Liddell won the admiration of the world in those Olympics because he refused to run on Sunday. He captured the imagination and hearts of millions by tossing away his chance of a gold medal in the 100 meters, the race in which he was the favorite, because he felt a principle of the Christian faith was more important than even the Olympic race.

After winning the medal and finding himself the toast of Scotland, Liddell quietly moved out of the limelight to become a missionary in China. When he died there as a prisoner of the Japanese nearly twenty years later, he was mourned in Britain as if he had never been away: "Scotland has lost a son who did her proud every hour of his life," wrote the *Glasgow Evening News.*

Abraham: Running with His Head Thrown Back

An interesting insight into Liddell's style of running and living is seen in the comments of Ian Charleson, who plays Eric in the inspiring film, *Chariots of Fire.* "Liddell's style was a problem," he said. "I had to learn to run properly and then to learn Liddell's way. The hardest thing was that Eric ran with his head back, but when I did it I couldn't see where I was going. I kept running off the track and bumping into other runners.

"Then one day, on the fifth or sixth day of filming, I suddenly cottoned on to what he must have been doing when he ran. At drama school we used to do what are called 'trust exercises,' where you run as hard as you can towards a wall and trust someone will stop you, or you fall off a piano and trust someone will catch you. I suddenly realized—Liddell must have run like that. He must have run with his head up and literally trusted to get there. He ran with faith. He didn't even look where he was going. So I see how that would have given him a lot of extra strength in a way. He just let go, completely relaxed."[1]

And that's what both Eric and Abraham did in their spiritual lives—they threw back their heads and ran in faith! Just listen to the writer of Hebrews as he describes how Abraham ran in faith:

> By faith, Abraham, when he was called to go out into a place which he should after receive for an inheritance, obeyed; and he went out, not knowing whither he went.
> By faith he sojourned in the land of promise, as in a strange country, dwelling in tabernacles with Isaac and Jacob, the heirs with him of the same promise.
> By faith Abraham, when he was tried, offered up Isaac: and he that had received the promises offered up his only begotten son, of whom it was said, That in Isaac shall thy seed be called (vv. 8-9, 17-18).

In Abraham we see the nature of faith and the depth of honest commitment. I think we see in Abraham something folks in our times are desperately wanting—a cause beyond themselves to which they can give their lives. A man who lives like Abraham inspires others to look at their own values and to become dissatisfied with playing around in the bathtub, calling themselves deep-sea fishermen!

Running with His Eyes on a Vision

If you yearn for a deeper meaning in your life, for a cause greater than your own selfish desires to which you can devote yourself, then listen carefully to the secret of Abraham's faith.

Turn first to the twelfth chapter of Genesis, in which Abraham first comes on the scene. God commands him to leave his home and his family, and in return promises him: "I will make of thee a great nation, and I will bless thee, and make thy name great ... and in thee shall all families of the earth be blessed" (vv. 2-3).

In the following chapter we learn of the dissension between the herdsmen of Abraham and his nephew, Lot. So, Lot is given his choice of the land, and Abraham will take what Lot doesn't want. It is in this context that God says to Abraham, "And I will make thy seed as the dust of the earth: so that if a man can number the dust of the earth, then shall thy seed also be numbered" (Gen. 13:16).

And in chapter 15 we see a renewal of God's promises to Abraham as the Lord said, "Fear not, Abram: I am thy shield, and thy exceeding great reward" (v. 1). To Abraham's reminder that, although God had promised to make him a mighty nation, he had no son and was old, God brought Abraham out of his tent and told him to look up at the evening sky: "Look now toward heaven, and tell the stars, if thou be able to number them: and he said unto him, So shall thy seed be" (v. 5). As part of this renewal of the covenant promises, God commanded Abraham to prepare a sacrifice of a young heifer, a female goat, a young ram, a dove, and a pigeon. "As the sun was going down, a great sleep fell upon Abram; and, lo, an horror of great darkness fell upon him" (v. 12). And in the still of that night, "behold a smoking furnace, and a burning lamp that passed between those pieces" (v. 17) of the sacrifice Abraham had arranged.

It is important to see that God called Abraham to be the recipient of the "blessing." That blessing was that he would be the "friend of God." The source of such a relationship was God himself. The blessing was to begin and operate in Abraham's own life, but it was to spread and reach on down to all nations, through his seed. The blessing itself was the possibility of being not an enemy of God, but God's friend.

Why That Man Ran Like That

The response of Abraham, and the commitment you and I make to God, must rest on some things we believe to be absolutely true without any shadow of a doubt.

Abraham believed *God was seeking him.* He felt that God had a plan for his life; something he wanted Abraham to do. Abraham didn't start the whole business—God did. In genuine turning to God, we find God is already, and always, there above and beside us. When Phillips Brooks, near the end of his life, was asked by a young clergyman what had been his secret, the most essential and striking part of Brooks's answer was this: "All experience comes to be but more pressure of His life on ours. . . . Less and less, I think grows the consciousness of seeking God. Greater and greater grows the certainty that He is seeking us and giving Himself to us to the complete measure of our present capacity."[2]

Abraham's faith was built on the solid conviction that *God was trustworthy* and would not lead him astray. Like Eric Liddell, Abraham ran with his head back because he trusted God to be with him, guiding and protecting. What Abraham had was not a contract with God, but a relationship which was far more useful. He was living by trust, not by sight. A recent TV commercial for a certain brand of glue illustrates the way Abraham did *not* live. The man in the advertisement expressed his confidence in the glue by putting his head into a frame and letting a heavy blade fall toward his exposed neck. At the last possible moment, the blade stopped in its swift descent, dramatically demonstrating the strength of the glue that held it. However, precautionary measures were taken for stopping the blade—just in case the glue failed to hold. Abraham's God was not in a box, neatly ribboned, but out ahead, beckoning Abraham onward. It is interesting to notice that while in Genesis "wandering" is a symbol of sin—as in the case with Cain—with Abraham it is a symbol of trust and faith:

> Alone with none but thee, My God
>   I journey on my way;
> What need I fear when thou art near,
>   O King of night and day?
> More safe am I within Thy hand than if
>   A host did round me stand.
>
> —Author Unknown

Abraham's faith rested squarely on his *obedience to the claims and demands of God.* Surely, as we will see, there must have been times when Abraham wondered why certain things happened, or why God acted in such a way—yet he obeyed. How we need to get a handle on obedience to God's demands. In our times we are so accustomed to our will being the center of the universe, and rationalizing away the demands of God, that we find it hard to march forward in obedience.

Paul Scherer gave me light on this matter of obedience to God in my own life as he told of a conversation with a friend about that age-old problem of human suffering. " 'Why does God allow it?' he [the friend] asked. 'This much I know,' he answered himself. 'I have seen a captain send one of his men, a dear friend of his, to certain death; and the man spent no time in asking why. He saluted and went. I do not know why, and I am not asking. I am just saluting, if that is my post. In God's name, can't we have the courage even of soldiers? He knows. So much I understand!' "[3] Every time I ponder that conversation my thoughts go to Tennyson's touching account of "The Charge of the Light Brigade":

> "Forward, the Light Brigade!"
> Was there a man dismayed?
> Not though the soldier knew
> Some one had blundered:
> Theirs not to make reply,
> Theirs not to reason why,
> Theirs but to do and die:
> Into the valley of death
> Rode the six hundred.

If soldiers can ride into the jaws of death, into the mouth of hell, is it asking too much of you and me, who have been redeemed from the mouth of hell, to be obedient? Can we not affirm that our God is wiser than we? Such was the foundation of faith which allowed Abraham to run with his head thrown back!

The Test of the Runner

It is fine and high-sounding to say such things, and they have the ring of idealism. But how does it work out in the life of the Christian? How did it work out in Abraham's life? Would he, did he, obey God? Chapter 22 of Genesis is an account of what would be the most horrible nightmare that any parent can possibly imagine. Abraham, after years of struggling to do God's will, after clinging to the promises in spite of what common sense would say, now felt God was telling him to sacrifice his son, his only son, whom he loved, the son of the promise—Isaac.

How did it come about? I do not have full insight into how Abraham came to the understanding that he must kill his son—it may well be that he had a dream or heard a voice. In any event, he came to that understanding and resolved to be faithful to the bitter end.

But it planted a dilemma deep in Abraham's heart. To *obey* what he felt was God's will for his life and his child meant losing the divine promise which was the cornerstone of his life, for the promise hinged on his son: "Tell the stars, if thou be able to number them: and he said unto him, So shall thy seed be" (Gen. 15:5). But to *disobey* this demand to kill his son, to be disobedient to what he felt was the will of God—that meant to forfeit the very basis on which the promise was made: "And he believed in the Lord; and he counted it to him for righteousness" (v. 6). He *must* obey.

Now our Bibles are not worried about some of the

modern aspects of this story as we view it. The question, "Why would God demand such?" is simply not asked. The possibility of Abraham misunderstanding God is not even entertained. The cruelty of such an act as slaying your own child is not mentioned. The protest of fatherly love is passed over in silence. And in a moment I will tell you why none of these considerations are at all important. But first, look at the scene.

The account in the twenty-second chapter is one of the most touching in the Old Testament. See how God calls Abraham to test him at the beginning of the story, and his brave reply is, "Here I am" (v. 1). Then, at the end, when his arm is raised to kill his son, God calls again, and again the brave reply is, "Here am I" (v. 11). Ready to obey at all times. Consider the picture of the silent man, silhouetted against a darkening sky toiling his tormented way up Mount Moriah, ready to obey God! I get a queasy feeling when I contrast that with the comfortable crowd sitting in cushioned pews complacently crooning "Ready to suffer grief or pain,/Ready to stand the test;/Ready to go, ready to stay,/Ready my place to fill;/Ready for service, lowly or great,/Ready to do his will."[4] See the gentle touch as the writer describes Isaac in three different ways, all showing Abraham's love for him: "Take now thy son, thine only son Isaac, whom thou lovest" (v. 2).

Abraham rises while it is still dark, dressing quietly so as not to awake Sarah, whom he has told that he and Isaac are going on a journey of some sort. Stooping at the entrance to Isaac's tent, he rouses him with a whisper, then goes over to the servants who have the donkey ready.

They travel three days, and with every pounding of the

donkey's hooves there is the pounding question in Abraham's brain, "Why Isaac? Why Isaac?" And on the third day he lifts up his eyes and beholds Mount Moriah, gaunt and wild, in the distance. Bidding his servants wait, Abraham loads the wood on his son and takes the pot of fire in one hand and the knife in the other, "they went both of them together" (v. 6). Isaac asks his father, "Behold the fire and the wood: but where is the lamb for a burnt offering?" (v. 7). And the reply of Abraham is one of deepest faith, "My son, God will provide himself a lamb for a burnt offering" (v. 8). "They went both of them together."

It is a powerful, emotional story as the camera ranges from the scene of an adventurer in faith leaving his home country to the face of a father as he raises the knife; from the majestic scene of God and Abraham staring at the star-studded sky and the promise of descendants like stars to the bewildering picture of God demanding that the promised son be slain on a barren rock.

At the last moment comes a cry from the sky, and the angel tells Abraham not to harm the boy, but instead to offer the sacrifice that God has indeed provided—a ram caught in the thicket behind him!

What the Runner Knows at the End of the Race

In the experience of Mount Moriah, Abraham learns some powerful and wonderful truths. First, that *our God is not like the pagan gods who require the death of what we love most.* Our God can bless without destroying our children; He desires for both us and our children a full and meaningful life. Jesus emphasized this truth by making the comparison between our love and care for our children, and God's love and care for us. "Or what man is there of you, whom if his son ask bread, will he give him a stone? Or if he ask a fish, will he give him a serpent? If ye then, being evil, know how to give good gifts unto your children, how much more shall your Father which is in heaven give good things to them that ask him? (Matt. 7:9-11).

There is a key to Abraham's spiritual growth as we think back over his walk with God. *He acted on the light he had, and in so doing, received more light for the journey.* That is what faith is all about—it is the "substance of things hoped for, the evidence of things not seen" (Heb. 11:1). In 1942, not long before his imprisonment by the Japanese, Eric Liddell wrote a book of prayers in which he said: "*Obedience* to God's will is the secret of spiritual knowledge and insight. It is not willingness to know, but willingness to *do* (obey) God's will that brings certainty."[5]

A fellow missionary to China, Annie Buchan, tells of Eric Liddell's last words as he lay dying on February 21, 1945. She was nursing him in his last hours and reported that he quietly said in a moment between seizures—"Annie, it's complete surrender." *Surrender.* Strange words for this hero to whisper with his last breath, some would say. But not really. Put it in the context of the faith in which he lived. He was doing what he did over and over in his life—surrendering himself to the God of Abraham, Isaac, and Jacob.

Would you live a life of victory, of faith, of spiritual adventure? You can as you cast your sins behind and open your heart in faith and trust to Jesus Christ. For He is the Lamb God has provided as the sacrifice for your sins and mine.

Remember, nobody stopped the hand of evil men on

that day when they stood on a hill near Moriah and killed the Lamb of God. Yet God is merciful to sinful men, and the blood of Jesus becomes our way to walk with God. Will you let the blood of the Lamb of God avail to cleanse you of your sins right now?

13
Ships and Havens
A Sermon for Youth
Proverbs 30:18-19

There be three things which are too wonderful for me, yea, four which I know not: The way of an eagle in the air; the way of a serpent upon a rock; the way of a ship in the midst of the sea; and the way of a man with a maid (Prov. 30:18-19).

"The way of a ship in the midst of the sea." Mankind has few fascinations more powerful than that of the ship. I discovered that early in my hobby of glassblowing. As a pastor in Georgia I used to take part in a local crafts fair twice a year. I would set up my equipment and display the glass items in one room of an old gristmill. All around the mill were craftsmen of various sorts from apple doll makers to blacksmiths to artists in oils. My booth was always surrounded by a crowd of folks fascinated by my glass creations: birds, animals, flowers, and ships. There is something magic and majestic about the tall masts and shimmering sails.

It seems that much of mankind has a running love affair with ships. We constantly speak of them in terms of the fairer sex. We persist in calling our airplanes "ships," and in the pioneer days of the West the settlers crossed the prairies in lumbering, cumbersome wagons which they called "prairie schooners"!

The Bible is full of stories about ships, even though the

Hebrews never were much as sailors. Men like former astronaut Jim Irwin are still searching for Noah's ship, even though it would be thousands of years old. Then there's Jonah's ship—the one in which he set sail to run away from God, and from which he was cast overboard into the sea, only to be swallowed by a huge fish and deposited back on dry land. And there are the disciples' boats or ships, depending on how big a ship has to be. And the ship from which Jesus stilled the storm on the Sea of Galilee one night. Then the Bible speaks of the ship in which Paul was being transported to Rome as a prisoner, and the storm that destroyed it, and the miraculous escape of all hands.

Not only do actual ships play an role in the Bible; ships are seen as a symbol of life: "[My days] are passed away as the swift ships: as the eagle that hasteth to the prey" (Job 9:26). Paul, in his first letter to Timothy, speaks of two men as having made shipwreck of their lives. Why does the Bible use such nautical imagery? And why are we so fascinated with ships?

Whither Bound?

We are so caught up with ships because *they are going somewhere.* Vacationing at the beach we see a beat-up, battered old freighter out on the horizon, and we wonder where in the seven seas that old tub has been. We can almost smell the sweet flowers of the South sea islands, and hear the soft wail of India's pipes, and feel the wind in our faces as we stand before the mast. Ships represent mystery and adventure. That's why boys will forever read *Treasure Island, Kidnapped,* and *Captains Courageous,* and why the *Mutiny On the Bounty* will never end.

And the first point of this message is this: *every person's life is like the voyage of a ship.* There is no more important question for every youth to ask himself—and none needing a clearer answer—than this: Where am I bound in life? I remember the childhood game, "My ship goes sailing . . ." The object was for the rest of the group to guess whither bound and with what cargo.

God's intention for your life is that it be a voyage, a pilgrimage, a journey to a definite destination. Norman Vincent Peale tells in one of his books about a rather interesting clipping from a newspaper that he picked up somewhere abroad. The heading reads: "Wears hollow in pub floor in 70 years." And it goes on to say, "Spalding, England: Jack East, 89, has made a lasting impression in the Pigeon Inn here. After 70 years as a regular drinker in the Lincolnshire pub, he has worn a hollow in the tiled floor. 'I must have bought enough pints to buy the place twice over,' says Mr. East, who used to quaff up to 20 pints of draught beer a day, but now limits himself to a couple at lunchtime. He has a regular spot by the bar which no one else uses. 'I've never drunk in any other pub and the only thing that has changed here is the price of beer.' In appreciation of his loyal drinking habits, the brewery that owns the 200-year-old tavern presented Jack with a five-gallon barrel of beer." Wouldn't you think that a fellow would do more in 70 years than wear a hole in the floor of a pub?

How tragic it is to see folks with no purpose, no destination in life. With the ancient mariner in Coleridge's poem they could say of their lives,

> Day after day, day after day,

> We stuck—nor breath nor motion;
> As idle as a painted ship
> Upon a painted ocean.

Perhaps almost as great a tragedy as not having a destination for your life, to be like a painted ship, is to be swept about by whatever winds are blowing in our society. The winds of drugs, rebellion, uncontrolled desires, and urges—these are not the gentle breezes of an idyllic life but rather the hurricane winds which can tear your life apart.

I remember the simple story of a young man who was visiting with an elderly friend. Finally the conversation got around to the boy's dreams for his life. "What do you plan to do in life?" asked the old man.

"I'll go to college and become a doctor or lawyer or something like that," said the boy.

"Then what?"

"Oh, I suppose I'll get married and begin to move up in my career."

"And then what?"

"Well, we'll raise a family and enjoy life."

"And then what?"

"Oh, I dunno—I guess we'll just get older like everybody else."

"And then what?"

"For Pete's sake—I suppose I'll die some day, but that's a long time off!"

"And then what?"

The cold truth is that *every life is going somewhere.* Jesus often spoke of the necessity to decide where you are going in life—you must choose between two masters, between two ways, between being a sheep or a goat, between heaven or hell. The choice is not *whether,* or *when*—only *where* we go with our lives.

The secret of the serene life is found in the knowledge of a chosen destination. In the fourteenth chapter of John's Gospel we see the power of knowing where your life is going. Jesus is twelve hours from the cross; from the terrible pain and humiliation of that disgraceful death. Is He lost in despair, disoriented from fear? Not at all.

See Him as He seeks to comfort His disciples who are sensing some sinister presence in their midst. The tension is heavy, and He who is about to die reassures those He leaves behind with the beautiful words: "Let not your heart be troubled: ye believe in God, believe also in me. In my Father's house are many mansions: if it were not so, I would have told you. I go to prepare a place for you" (John 14:1-2).

The reason Jesus had such peace even in the face of death is found in the direction of His life; in His relationship to the Father. For in the account of the supper which preceded the beautiful words about the Father's mansion, we read: "Jesus knowing that the Father had given all things into his hands, and that he was come from God, and went to God" (John 13:3).

Jesus knew where He had come from, and where He was bound. Secure in that knowledge, His heart was at rest. Do you have that kind of peace in your life? Do you know where your life is bound? Do you know your destination if you were to sail away from this world today? Listen, we have no assurance of tomorrow! Paul gives us a lovely word picture in Philippians 1:23 as he contemplates his possible death at the hands of the Romans: "For I am in a strait betwixt two, having a desire to depart, and to be with Christ; which is far better." The Greek word translated "depart" in this verse is often used to speak of pulling up anchor, setting sail on a voyage. Can you speak with Paul's certainty about the destination of your life, or must the prayer of the fearful be yours: An unknown poet expressed it:

> Through trackless seas I plow my way,
> By unnamed stars I steer;
> No rudder guides my chartless drift,
> No compass holds me true—
> O Master of this helpless ship;
>   Have mercy on the crew!

What Is Your Cargo?

The second question every person, and especially youth, ought to ask themselves is, "What is the cargo, the meaning, the influence, the purpose of my life?" Every time I see a painting of an old Viking ship, or a Spanish galleon of the Armada, or an English frigate or Clipper under sail, I wonder—"What's her cargo?" Not long ago I read of a man who spent seventeen years seeking the sunken wreck of a ship which was part of the Spanish treasure fleet which sank in a hurricane north of the Dominican Republic in 1641. And after a seventeen-year search the man finally found the sunken hulk. And, would you believe it, the wreck is filled with enough gold to ransom ten kings! A ship with a priceless cargo.

On the other hand, I suppose many ships contain nothing of much value. On my first visit to the seashore, my father, as I remember, told me why the sea was salty. He explained that once upon a time there was a little man who had a marvelous invention—a salt-making machine. Only problem was, he had no way to turn off the machine! Soon the kitchen table on which it sat was overflowing with salt, then the whole house, and then the salt piled out into his yard. Everybody in the village began to gripe, and he had to leave, taking his machine with him. Boarding a ship, he thought to go far away, but as the machine continued to make salt, soon the ship was overloaded and sank to the bottom of the sea! That's right, the machine is down there somewhere, in that sunken hull, still making salt!

I don't vouch for either the treasure story or the salt story. But I do think that the cargo of a ship would determine its destination, don't you? What cargo does your life carry? In other words, *what is the meaning of your life?* What do you think about the most? What shapes your life? What do you spend most of your time doing or dreaming about? What things have the most influence on you?

The eloquent preacher and writer, Henry Van Dyke, once commented there are only four cargos in a person's life: *fame, fortune, pleasure,* and *usefulness to God.* Fame is so fleeting. By the time you get to the end of life's voyage, both you and most others will have forgotten the fame you struggled so hard to attain.

The man once known as "Pistol Pete," Pete Maravich, says there was little joy in his ten-year National Basketball Association career. "I love basketball, I was dedicated to basketball, and it was fun to an extent in college," the former LSU All-American and NBA All-Star said after he was recently inducted into the Louisiana Sports Hall of Fame. "But it was never the joy it should have been . . . because I wouldn't let it . . . I was obsessed," he said. "The ring became a god to me . . . now, when I look back on it, I almost can't believe how important it was to me!"[1]

Fortune is also a poor investment for eternity. I dare say that this world holds nothing of material value which will be worth much in heaven. And, after all, wealth is a matter of perception. Some cultures value seashells and bits of bone above all else. And pleasure—how easily it is distorted and twisted, and how fleeting it is. Most of our pleasure is merely the sucking on a damp washrag to soothe our thirst for eternal things.

Van Dyke's fourth cargo is the only one which is always worthwhile: *usefulness to God.* And this cannot be achieved to its fullest unless you have a saving relationship to God through Christ. Paul remarks in Philippians that all those things which used to have value for him he now counted as garbage, in order to gain the knowledge and fellowship of Jesus: to have a usefulness to God.

Look at it like this. In my library are thousand of books —big books and little books, long books and short books, good books and bad books, fancy books and plain books. But the books which are the most useful to me—underlined, dog-eared and worn—are the most valuable. These are the ones which have fulfilled their purpose. I really want to be such a book in God's library!

Will You Reach Your Destination?

My family used to vacation on the Outer Banks of North Carolina. One of its fascinations for us was its ghost fleet. Over the past 350 years, a thousand ships have come to their ruin on these inshore waters around the Outer

Banks. Six hundred of these wrecks are well documented. The ghost fleet of the Atlantic constitutes ships that never made it to their destination.

Will you make it to your destination? Or will your life be in shambles by middle age? How sad to see young people load their lives with worthless cargo, and then to see them crack up on the shoals of life. But it is inevitable in a time when so many have no morals, no ideals, no daily walk with Jesus.

There is no possibility of your reaching God's intended destination of a full and meaningful life both here and in heaven—unless Jesus is your guide: "Jesus, Saviour, pilot me/Over life's tempestuous sea. . . . " For all have sinned; the flaw is already there in the rudder; the boat already leaks; and the wages of our sin is death.

People sometimes make *shipwreck of their lives through fear of sailing out into the deep with God.* Many of those ships which sank on the Diamond Shoals of the Outer Banks of North Carolina did so because they tried to stay too close to shore. They felt too attached to the familiar; they lacked the spirit of adventure.

Some folks make *shipwreck of their lives through mutiny.* We were made for fellowship with God, and through Jesus the great gap between God and man is bridged. It is spiritual mutiny to turn your back and heart on the cross of Jesus, and will surely make shipwreck of your life.

The Harbor of the Heavenly Home

The writer of the Proverbs spoke of the beauty and mystery of a ship in the midst of the sea. And there is still little, I suppose, to surpass the mystique of a trim ship, white sails, and blue sea.

What a tremendous way to think of a soul at home on the sea of life because Jesus is the captain of that soul. Who runs your life? Where are you going? Can you be honest enough to admit that you've loaded some of the wrong cargo? Can you admit that you're headed for the wrong destination?

As a college student, one of my favorite pictures was the familiar one of a young person at the helm of a ship in a storm. The waves tower above the frail craft, the youth is soaked with spray, lightning splits the dark sky, and the wind rages. But standing behind the youth is the Master of the storms of life, Jesus Christ. And He stands ready this day to guide your life.

>O Maker of the Mighty Deep
>   Whereon our vessels fare,
>Above our life's adventure keep
>   Thy faithful watch and care.
>In Thee we trust, whate'er befall
>Thy sea is great, our boats are small.
>
>We know not where the secret tides
>   Will help us or delay,
>Nor where the lurking tempest hides,
>   Nor where the fogs are gray.
>We trust in Thee, whate'er befall:
>Thy sea is great, our boats are small.
>
>Beyond the circle of the sea,
>   When voyaging is past,
>We seek our final port in Thee;
>   O bring us home at last.

In Thee we trust, whate'er befall
Thy sea is great, our boats are small.

—Henry Van Dyke

14
Christ at the Door
Revelation 3:14-22

Behold, I stand at the door, and knock: if any man hear my voice, and open the door, I will come in to him (Rev. 3:20).

It is difficult for a passage of Scripture to speak with equal force to the hearts of both the church and the unbeliever. Yet, that is exactly what this text does. Verse 20 of our passage of Scripture says, "Behold, I stand at the door, and knock: if any man hear my voice, and open the door, I will come in to him, and will sup with him, and he with me."

Christ at the door—a powerful image and a powerful truth, both for the believer and the unbeliever. The background of the text itself concerns Christ at the door of the church, and so we shall first consider the strange sight of Christ knocking on the door of His own church!

The Excluded Christ

Consider with me the excluded Christ. Now, there is nothing strange or odd about His exclusion from certain places: the local atheist meeting, the girlie show houses, the hangout of the drug peddlers—the Satan-dominated places. But Christ shut out from His own church? Yet that is the scene in the text.

At the beginning of the Book of Revelation we find a

marvelous description of Christ walking in the midst of His churches. This scene in chapter 1, verses 12 through 20, came alive for me some years ago when a group of us ministers were driving from Florida to our annual Southern Baptist Convention meeting in Denver, Colorado. While going through the Texas panhandle we ran into one of the heaviest rainstorms I have ever experienced. We pulled off the road to wait out the storm, keeping our eyes on the blue-black sky.

Then, on the western horizon we saw a glow in the dark sky. When we could continue driving slowly, the glow remained in the darkening sky as evening came on. We finally drew nearer and discovered the glow came not from fires set by lightning, but were the giant torches of an oil refinery, burning off waste gases. What a majestic sight atop great torches, the flames leaped fifty feet into the dark sky, lighting up the sky with a glow seen miles away!

Just so the churches are represented as blazing torches which light up this world of darkness. And walking among the churches, seen by the light of the churches, is the Christ. A central theme of the New Testament is the presence and communion of Christ with His churches. Yet, here is a dreadful thought—the idea of Christ standing outside, knocking on the door of His own church!

It it possible that Christ could be *outside* our church, while we present the music, the sermons, the prayers to *ourselves?* Now that we think about it, have we really needed Him lately anyhow? Like "Old What's His Name" who hasn't been to church in years but who hasn't been missed, would we even notice the absence of Christ? Have we done anything lately at our church that a group of pagans with the same resources could not have accomplished? Have we, as a church, felt His presence lately?

Why Is He Standing Outside?

What's He doing out there? The key to why Christ just might be standing outside the closed door of many churches is found in what we know of the church in our text—the church at Laodicea.

This was a wealthy city. When a great earthquake struck the region in Paul's day, Rome had to rebuild most of the cities in the area, but not Laodicea. This city, named for the wife of the Emperor Claudius, was at the convergence of three major highways. A hub of commerce, the big apple of the Lycus Valley. There were three major industries: wool, banking, and medicine.

The church in Laodicea? A reflection of the city, as most churches have a tendency to be! Otherwise, we know it was a church free from major theological error. No accusing these folks of such sins or Jezebels as plagued Philadelphia, or Thyatira, or Pergamos, or Sardis. No, they wouldn't put up with false doctrine any longer than a mongoose and a cobra could live together.

Their chief downfall was their wealth. By the world's standards and their own assessment they were rich. And their wealth and ease led to independence. Notice verse 17: "I am rich, and increased with goods, and have need of nothing."

This led to three results. First, they developed a *false understanding of themselves.* If you visited that church, they would play "show and tell" with their buildings and numbers. If you were to suggest they were bound by complacency; that they desperately needed a season of revival, repentance, and prayer, they would be both astonished and offended. Jesus asserted they were afflicted, miserable, poor, blind, naked—words of pity!

The second result of their condition of wealth and ease was *lukewarmness*. Lukewarmness: a spiritual condition in which conviction does not affect the conscience, the heart, or the actions! The cross was not denied; it just was not vital.

The word *zeal* is used to translate the Greek word meaning "boil." Zeal: that part of our commitment to Christ which, when left out, makes us useless to the kingdom of Christ. I fear some churches resemble the huge jigsaw puzzle of the advertisement in a store window. The sign said: "Huge Jigsaw Puzzle Bargain—Was $39.95, now only $2.95." In small letters below was printed this explanation: "three pieces missing"! It may be that only zeal is missing in your church, but if so—it is well-night worthless as a true church!

Lukewarmness is a contradiction of all a church professes. How can a church be lukewarm and really believe that every person is a sinner, bound for hell unless his life is changed? How can the lukewarm church really confess that Jesus died to save sinners? There is a contradiction between the lukewarm church and the urgency of the gospel message!

And so the church in Laodicea shut Christ out. In their blindness and nakedness, all they could see was gold, and they tried to clothe themselves with pride. How sad that the Creator and Lord of the church should have to say of Himself, "Behold, I stand at the closed door of the church!" (author).

Will He Come In?

When we tell Jesus by our actions He is not wanted or needed, that He interferes with our life-style or church-style, He leaves. He will not return to a church until we hear His voice and open the door. He will not come in until we "boil" and repent of our complacency and lukewarmness.

The Excluded Christ Again

The background of our text demands that we see the reality of the church excluding Christ, but that does not mean the power of this verse is limited to that usage only. The Holy Spirit has often seen fit to use this verse about the closed door to convict the unsaved person.

Christ at the door! The artist Holman Hunt has a famous painting on this theme—in fact, he painted two copies of the same picture on this theme. One hangs in Oxford and the other in St. Paul's in London. This picture, copies of which you've no doubt seen, is a marvelous portrait of Christ knocking at a closed door. In fact, the picture is on the cover of this book.

Christ is portrayed as prophet, priest, and king—wearing the white robe of the prophet, the breastplate of the priest, and the king's crown of golden thorns. There are two sources of light in the painting: His face gently shines with a warm, soft light—the pleading of the Savior. In His hand He holds a lantern, the lantern of conscience and of God's Word.

And what is shown in the light of the lantern of conscience as He stands before the door? A door covered with cobwebs, with rusty hinges, and nailed shut. Ivy and vines creep up the door. The path to the door is overgrown with weeds, and in the circle barely lit by the lantern, we can see a bat, the symbol of darkness. There is also an apple, half hidden, the symbol of man's rebellion from God. It is a piercing picture of man locking God out. The excluded Christ of the individual heart!

Behind the Door of the Heart

If Hunt has painted a marvelous picture of the Christ outside the door of our hearts pleading entrance, an equally probing word portrait of that heart behind the door has been penned by Paul in the first chapter of Romans. In verses 18 through 32, Paul describes that heart as deserving the wrath of a rightous God. Our hearts—for Paul is speaking of you and me—are darkened because although we know God, we have a tendency not to praise and love Him.

In this darkest of all passages in the Bible, God says we worship the creature—ourselves—rather than Him who made us. The passage ends with a catalog of the kind of sin that infects the minds, hearts, and bodies of us all—sexual sins, spiritual sins, and sins which lock the door of our rebellious hearts. The list of the symptoms of our proud and vicious rebellion against God closes with the assertion that, although the just reward of those who do such things is known to us, we not only do them, but also sit on the fence and applaud others as they shake their fists at Almighty God!

Paul's terrible indictment of us sinners in Romans 1 is followed up by the ringing pronouncements of Romans 3:23, "For all have sinned, and come short of the glory of God", and Romans 6:23, "For the wages of sin is death." The Bible is based on the second surest fact in all the world: we are sinners. (If you wonder what the surest fact in all the world is—it is the fact that God loves sinners!) Every human being is a sinner. Young or old, boy or girl, wise or foolish, rich or poor, black or white—sinners all.

Someone will say, "We can't *all* be spiritually sick!" Yes, we can and we are! It may seem odd in the classroom when *all* the pupils fail the test, but this is exactly what has happened in the school of life. All four billion (plus) of us on the planet earth are sinners!

The root of the matter is that everybody is born with a tendency toward self-love, toward self-rule. We want to love ourselves more than God, and we want to try to run our lives. Think for a moment if you have babies at your house, or have ever observed them much. Now, a baby hasn't done any of the things you may associate with sin—robbing banks, running off with someone's husband or wife, murdering somebody. Yet everybody is a sinner according to the Bible —even that sweet little bundle of joy. How can that be?

My wife and I have pondered the fact that when our children were babes, they loved chocolate pudding. Got that naturally. And we would try to feed them the chocolate pudding. If they would have just opened their mouths, we would have filled them to the brim with that goody. But they wouldn't. A chubby hand would grab the spoon, turn it over and watch the pudding splatter on the floor, or flip the spoon as they smiled like an angel while pudding plopped onto the ceiling, or in our faces, or on their heads. It was a manifestation of an inner tendency to do it themselves—to run their own lives. It is the root of selfishness, of jealousy, of greed, and overleaping ambition—this desire to have no master, no lord, nobody running our lives. That's sin in its simplest form.

I tell boys and girls that they are born with that tendency to push God away, to run their own lives, but to do what comes naturally is to live a life in which God has no part and which will eventually end in sorrow and death! I tell the children, "You may, at the end of your life, be a very famous woman or a very rich man, but you will not be happy if you have not let Jesus come into your life and guide you."

Who at My Door Is Standing?

Who is this Jesus that stands at every heart's door? What right has He to want control of my life? The Bible may best be divided, for our understanding of salvation history, not as Old and New Testaments, but rather into these two portions: Genesis 1 through 11, and Genesis 12 through the Book of Revelation!

The first part of the Bible tells us of God's original intention in creation, the beneficent provisions He made for us, and the turning of the first couple in rebellion from God. The second part of the Bible tells us how God did not give up on His rebellious creation but chose a people to be His very own "treasure," and partners in calling this wicked world back to God. The story winds its way through the Old Testament and shows us how God worked with this imperfect people whom He had chosen; calling them out of Egypt, raising up prophets, guiding their nation when allowed. But the bald truth is that those whom God chose did not want the glorious privilege of being God's partners in re-creation of this wrecked world. So God took upon Himself the mantle of flesh and became one of us—Jesus of Nazareth.

The reason Jesus came to earth was to call us to God, to plead with us all to repent of our wicked attitudes and ways and let God guide our hearts. His death on the cross shows us to what lengths our evil nature will go, and to what lengths God's love will go.

All through these centuries since Jesus died on the cross, God's Holy Spirit has been confronting sinners like you and me with that cross and the love of God nailed there. And blessed is the man who, like Christian in *The Pilgrim's Progress,* realizes that "he hath given me rest by his sorrow, and life by his death."

Surely you have noticed the growth rings in a recently cut tree stump. While studying a dark spot in the middle of the rings of such a stump, I realized that the dark spot went from top to bottom of that tree, although I could see only a cross-section. So it is with the cross. Where we are, and where we experience the cross, is only a cross-section of God's love and suffering for us—the cross extends through all of history and for every person in the world.

One of the most heartbreaking stories of the horrors of World War II is that of Anne Frank, a young Jewish girl who, with her family, perished in the gas chambers. Her diary tells of the terror that always accompanied any knock at the door of their hiding place. Was it a friend bringing food or the Gestapo bringing death? There was a world of meaning in a simple knock.

There is one who knocks this day at your heart's door, a friend, bearing the mark of the nails and offering you not death, but life eternal. Some have said Hunt's picture of this Christ at your door is not finished—for there is no door handle. But it *is* finished; the handle is on the inside! You must open the door of your heart.

> Knocking, knocking, who is there?
> Waiting, waiting, oh, how fair!
> 'Tis a Pilgrim, strange and kingly,
> Never such was seen before.
> Ah! my soul, for such a wonder
> Wilt thou not undo the door?
>
> Knocking, knocking, still He's there,
> Waiting, waiting, wondrous fair;
> But the door is hard to open,
> For the weeds and ivy-vine,
> With their dark and clinging tendrils,
> Ever round the hinges twine.
>
> Knocking, knocking—what, still there?
> Waiting, waiting, grand and fair;
> Yes, the pierced hand still knocketh,
> And beneath the crowned hair
> Beam the patient eyes, so tender,
> Of thy Saviour, waiting there.
>
> —Mrs. H. B. Stowe

15
One Life, One Death, One Account
Genesis 5:21-29

And Enoch walked with God: and he was not; for God took him (Gen. 5:24).

I remember an old saying from childhood days in North Florida. Packed with meaning, it runs like this:

> One life to live,
> One death to die,
> One account to give.

And how true that old expression is when we pause to ponder the parts of it. *One life to live*—in spite of all the talk of reincarnation. One life to live—and only one—regardless of the dreams of the pitiful human bundles wrapped in tinfoil in a freezer outside of Los Angeles. Poor people, unwilling to accept their mortality, they hope to continue an earthly life through "cryogeny," the science of refrigeration. And so they wait for a future generation to unlock the mysteries of life and death, cure whatever ailed them, and call them from their cold resting places!

One death to die, and that death laughs at all our vain efforts to hold it back. Bryant's *Thanatopsis* still rings true with its description of the "innumerable caravan which moves/To that mysterious realm where each shall take/His chamber in the silent halls of death." All the undertaker's art cannot change the reality and certainty of death or bring the dead to life for one moment.

One account to give—in spite of our rejection of God. For men have always felt there is a responsibility to life, and man must give an answer to something—someone—for the living of it.

An Old Saying Full of Questions

Each segment of this old saying raises questions we cannot ignore, cannot run away from.

One life to live: what will I do with mine? What will I seek? Will my life be successful? *Is* my life successful? What is *success?* How will I measure whether or not my life is successful?

One death to die: we know it's coming; but Daffy, our Siamese cat, doesn't. Why do we as humans know death is our lot, but the animals don't? While I don't have all the answers, I know this much—that the knowledge of impending death gives a perspective to our lives. We know we *will* die, but not *when*.

What kind of death will you die? By that I do not mean, will you die with your boots on, or die in bed of pneumonia, or be hanged as a horse thief—but *will your death have meaning?* If you died today, would your death have meaning for you or anyone else? Spiritual meaning?

One account to give. We are becoming more and more aware of the stewardship nature of life. In relation to the family of nations, America is finding we cannot continue indefinitely to be the world's policeman. At the same time we are beginning to hear the cries of starving children halfway round the world—not loudly, but at least we hear them. In relation to the natural world we are beginning to realize the terrible pollution of the environment and the finite nature of our energy resources. Scientists are telling us that wanton destruction of the world's tropical rain forests will impact a little old lady in Memphis, and may even raise the temperature of the entire world. Traditional enemies among nations are beginning to sit down at the conference table, realizing that we are all living together in a fragile world.

In relation to the spiritual world, how sad to see a person deny his stewardship of life before Almighty God! Have we decided there is no squaring of the account after this life? No righting of wrongs, no avenging the blood of the downtrodden and the innocent? Is man more concerned with right and wrong, with his worldly law courts, than Almighty God is?

Three Pegs for Life, Death, and Judgment

This old saying,

> One life to live,
> One death to die,
> One account to give,

will come alive if we can use three Old Testament characters as pegs on which to hang our thoughts:

> One life to live: Methuselah
> One death to die: Enoch, Methuselah's Dad
> One account to give: Noah

Methuselah is an approprite peg on which to hang our thoughts about life since he lived so long—969 years. His father, Enoch, is the peg for assessing death since "he was not; for God took him." And Methusaleh's grandson, Noah, will be our peg on which we hang our thoughts about judgment.

One Life to Live

So many things in this life are so unequal! So few of us have the talent of Paul Newman, Picasso, Beethoven, or James Michener. Most of us aren't nearly as beautiful as Bo Derek or Linda Gray. There are so few Einsteins among us, and none of the 500 names on the list of the richest persons in the world are among my personal acquaintances. In the midst of so many inequities—talent, beauty, fame, fortune—we are all equal in having *one life*. And there is a terrible weight in the realization that my life is *my* life. It is not my parents' life, not my teachers' life, not my wife's life, not my children's life—nor even my church member's life—it is *mine*. If I let them run it, or even ruin it, it is still *my* life, the only one I have.

Let us each one look inside his heart now, and examine one's own life. What dimensions does your life have? Does it merely have *length* or does it have *depth?* If anybody could be considered an authority on length of life, it was certainly Methuselah.

Think about Methuselah for a moment. Do you suppose he started out to live to be a thousand? Did he refuse to play ball or run or climb trees for fear of getting hurt? Did he eat all the right foods, brush his teeth, look both ways before crossing the streets, and always wear his rubbers when it rained? Perhaps, and he would have made it to 1,000—if he hadn't been caught in the flood! Methuselah was drowned in the great flood! The years are given in chapter 5 of Genesis—count 'em!

It is not enough to pattern after Methuselah. He had length of life—but not depth. As a student in Southeastern Seminary, located on the old Wake Forest College campus in Wake Forest, North Carolina, I was always impressed by a large plaque on the wall of what was then Johnson Hall. The plaque read:

<blockquote>
William Amos Johnson
1902-25
Professor Physician Christian Friend
"He Wrote His Life on a Shining Page"
</blockquote>

Only twenty-three years—but look at the meaning and depth in the titles of the plaque! A Christian, a professor, a physician, a friend to students—all by the age of twenty-three, and then to die. Yet I think this man truly lived more than Methuselah.

Consider David Brainerd. His years: 1718-47. Only twenty-nine years. Betrothed to Johnathan Edwards's daughter but swept away by death before marriage; missionary to the Indians of New England for only two years, with a total of no more than eighty-five converts. Who really tasted deepest of life, Methuselah at 969 or David Brainerd at twenty-nine? John Wesley directed all his preachers to read carefully the life of Brainerd, and William Carey, the father of modern missions and translator of the Scriptures into forty languages and dialects, pointed to Brainerd as his inspiration. Truly he embodied the words of Charles Kingsley:

> The very air teems thick with leagued fiends;
> Each word we speak has infinite effects;
> Each soul we pass must go to heaven or hell . . .
> Be earnest, earnest, earnest—*mad* and thou wilt:
> Do what thou doest as if the stake were heaven
> And this thy last deed ere the judgment day.

Or think upon William Borden, known to another generation as "Borden of Yale." Born with the proverbial silver spoon in his mouth, Borden was converted and gave his life to missions. While a college and seminary student he worked with the underprivileged, and upon graduation from seminary set upon a course of missionary work. While in language study in Cairo, Egypt, he fell ill and died. He was buried in foreign soil while the Moslem grave diggers stood by and watched the tiny missionary band lift their voices in the closing hymn:

> Sing it softly through the gloom,
>   When the heart for mercy craves;
> Sing in triumph o'er the tomb,
>   Jesus saves! Jesus saves!
>
>   —Priscilla Owens

His death? At the age of twenty-six. But "he wrote his life on a shining page," as Mrs. Howard Taylor put it her book, *Borden of Yale '09.*

Not Length But Depth

It is not length that gives meaning to life, but depth. And the deepest meaning in life is found in our relationship to God. That is why you cannot ignore Jesus of Nazareth, who we as Christians believe to be the very Son of God, and the only mediator between man and God. Jesus is no vague figure like Beowulf; Bethlehem is no fabled spot like Camelot. City bus number 22 travels to Bethlehem from Jerusalem every half hour, crowded with everything from collards to tourists. Many of us declare that Jesus is the mainspring of our life. As one of us put it nearly 2000 years ago: "For me to live is Christ" (Phil. 1:21).

There is no such thing as a free life; no such thing as "running my own life." Every life is guided, shaped, dominated by something or someone. And this is the burden of the Bible: that your *one life* have meaning, whether you live to be 969 or sixty-nine or thirty-nine or nineteen. That you not waste it and find in the light of eternity that you built on the wrong foundation and the house crumbled; you amassed a fortune but couldn't take it with you; you were known to millions but did not know God. As the poem so aptly says: "only one life, 'twil soon be past; only what's done for Christ will last."

> One life to live,
> One death to die,
> One account to give.

One Death to Die

Death is the inescapable fact which gives meaning to life. It gives a perspective—to some folks a perspective of hopelessness and despair. To others the perspective is one of hope and courage.

Death is *inevitable*. "It is appointed unto men once to die" (Heb. 9:27). Everybody you have ever known either has died or will die, unless Jesus returns first. And an important question is, "What kind of death will it be?" What will be the internal meaning of our death?

Consider a young man, only thirty-three, nailed to a cross to die, then spat upon and cursed while he suffered under the searing sun. Finally he leaned his fevered head against the rough cross and whispered: "Father, forgive them; for they know not what they do" (Luke 23:34).

Contrast that picture with the account of the short story writer William Porter, better known as O. Henry, as he lay dying at the close of day. As the shadows lengthened both outside and within his life, he called a nurse in the twilight and begged for a candle to be lit, for, said he: "I'm afraid to go home in the dark!"

Will Your Death Be in Faith or Fear?

Each one of us can live whatever years are given to us with a depth that takes the sting, the power away from our death. It all depends upon our relationship to God.

It is beautifully illustrated in one little girl's explanation of how "[Enoch] was not, for God took him." "It was like this," said the little girl. "Enoch and God were walking and talking one afternoon and completely lost track of time.

When suddenly they noticed the time of day, Enoch was far from home and said, 'I better get going, or it will be dark before I get home.' So God just said to him, 'Enoch, it's closer to my home than to go back to yours—come on home with me.'" How you interpret death depends upon your relationship with God. "While I draw this fleeting breath,/ When mine eyes shall close in death,/When I rise to worlds unknown,/And behold thee on thy throne,/Rock of Ages, cleft for me, Let me hide myself in thee." The Christian can say with Paul, "O death, where is thy sting? O grave, where is thy victory?" (1 Cor. 14:55).

> One life to live,
> One death to die,
> One account to give.

One Account to Give

Now let me be theological. Pagans can, and do, frame life and death without any reference to faith in God. Some folks can give moralistic advice without any reference to God. But the clear word of the Bible compels me to say bluntly, all unbelief not withstanding, that we will all give an account to God for the way we have lived this earthly life.

"It is appointed unto men once to die, but after this the judgment." In Matthew 13 Jesus says we shall account for every idle word. Paul in Romans 14 says "we shall all stand before the judgment seat of Christ," and "every one of us shall give account of himself to God" (vv. 10, 12). Our final, ultimate account will not be given to the Internal Revenue Service, nor to a civic club, nor even to a church or a pastor, but to Almighty God alone.

How shall we give an acceptable account of our lives to God? Sir Walter Scott asked:

> That day of wrath, that dreadful day,
> When heaven and earth shall pass away,
> What power shall be the sinner's stay?
> How shall he meet that dreadful day?

Consider the third man of our trio of Old Testament characters: Noah, the grandson of Methuselah. Think for a moment about Noah. We generally see him as a man who acted in circumstances which will never be repeated. At least, we trust the rainbow sign that the world will never be flooded again. But to tie Noah to the actual flood that way misses the point of the Bible here. Noah's example of faith lies not in riding out the flood in the ark—but in the *building* of it. In his quiet trust that, in the midst of corruption, God was alive and well and still in control, he lived a life of faith and worship, and was able to hear God above all the uproar of sin.

The tragic aspect of Noah's life is in his rejected testimony. He could hear God, but the neighbors neither *could* hear God nor *would* hear Noah as he warned them and began to build the ark.

This past summer I saw an incident in the old city of Nordlingen, Germany, which reminds me of Noah. Nordlingen's old Saint George Church with its "Daniel" tower is the focus and center of the town. Every night from 10 PM until 2 AM the watchman in the tower cries out the time hourly, on the hour. It has been done for centuries. So, staying at a little hotel in the shadow of the church, I came out to the street at 11 PM and stood with a dozen or so other visitors to see this tradition. Craning our necks, we stared up at the floodlit tower.

High up was a little, lighted window, and we anxiously waited for the clock to strike and the watchman to open the shutters, stick his head out, and cry out the hour. The clock struck, the window was opened, the man opened his mouth for a few seconds—and then turned back inside and shut the window. And we had not heard a word—for a motorcycle came roaring by at the exact moment he spoke his words far up in the tower! There was something futile about his efforts to be heard above the roar of the village below.

I think that's the way Noah's pleadings got lost. He had a message, because he followed God, but it couldn't be heard. Consider his relationship to God. First, Noah *listened* to God rather than men. God told him to build the ark. Apparently he lived far from the sea, and the people laughed at the foolish man and his ark. "There's a flood a-coming!" The foolish people laughed and mocked. He heard voices they couldn't hear; he marched to a different drummer.

Then Noah *trusted* God to bring to pass what He said. After all, it wasn't raining when Noah started to build. What made Noah listen and trust God? What is the difference in his relationship to God and the relationship his grandfather, Methuselah, had with God? Was it the stories of his great-grandfather, Enoch, told around the fires at night that stirred his soul to walk with God, too? We can never know what was the stairway to God in Enoch's life or in Noah's. But there was one, and climbing that stairway, opening up their lives to God, made all the difference.

What will you do with your life? What will be the

meaning of your death? What kind of account will you be able to give to God? Guilty sinners find a forgiven life through faith in Jesus Christ. Lonely, empty sinners find a deep and meaningful life through trusting Jesus. Will you trust Him as your Lord and Savior right now?

> One life to live,
> One death to die,
> One account to give.

16
A Stairway to God
Genesis 28:12-22

And he dreamed, and behold a ladder set up on the earth, and the top of it reached to heaven: and behold the angels of God ascending and descending on it (Gen. 28:12).

His nickname: "Root 'em out!"

His game: get ahead at any cost; climb the ladder of ambition, stand at the top, and wave at the poor suckers below.

This description could be of you, or of the next person you meet on the street. The truth is, this is a description of Abraham's grandson, Jacob. But the Bible is like an old family photo album, in which you can see Grandpa, Aunt Sally, Cousin Sam, and yourself.

It seems clear to me that God's intention in the Book of Genesis has little to do with explaining the creation of the world, but plenty to do with explaining man's sinful nature (chs. 1—11), and setting forth God's remedy for that fatal condition (ch. 12 to the end of the Bible).

And that is why no story in the Old or New Testaments is there simply for biographical or historical sake, but to illustrate and underline either the bitter facts of our lostness and our sinful nature or the provisions of God's salvation and the nature and life of God's people. As we look at the life of Jacob, the first actors on the stage are a doting, deceived father; a scheming mother; a tricked elder brother, Esau; and the spoiled mother's darling, Jacob. To describe him so is to barely scratch the surface of his character. His down-to-earth nature, practical bent, and makeup as a mercenary, cunning scoundrel first appears at his birth! We are told that when he and his twin brother, Esau, were born, Jacob was the second to emerge from the womb and came forth with a hand grasping his brother's heel.

We pick up the story on that day when the father Isaac —old, blind, and close to death—calls Esau to him. Now Esau was a hairy, red-faced hunter, an outdoorsman. His father urges him to go hunting and prepare some venison broth, and upon eating it Isaac will bestow the family blessing upon Esau as his eldest son.

But walls have ears, and the scheming mother, Rebekah, hurries to her favorite son, Jacob. She tells him to fetch a young goat, which she will prepare while he puts the skins on his arms and neck. Sure enough, when Jacob, pretending to be Esau, brings the broth, the blind old man cannot tell the difference between his sons, and feeling the rough, hairy arms of Jacob removes what suspicions he may have had. In this incident, we see Jacob lie twice concerning his identity, and then lie about God: "Isaac said unto his son, How is it that thou has found it so quickly, my son? And he [Jacob] said, Because the Lord thy God brought it to me" (Gen. 27:20). Notice, "*thy* God brought it to me."

The inevitable happened. Exit the scoundrel, enter the son Esau. We can imagine the old man's consternation and Esau's bitter disappointment as the trick is discovered. "Who art thou? And he said, I am thy son, thy firstborn Esau. And Isaac trembled very exceedingly" (v. 33). When he tells Esau what has transpired a few minutes before, Esau "cried with a great and exceeding bitter cry, and said unto his father, Bless me, even me also, O my father" (v. 34). But the feeble substitute blessing is but a blessing of servitude to his brother Jacob.

And so the curtain falls on the first scene with Esau full of hatred for his brother, the father Isaac with darkness in both his eyes and his heart, and the deceiver Jacob on the run.

Now, the bothersome thought about this scoundrel Jacob is that God's plan to bless the world rests on him and his kind! How can he be a blessing? Yet he has the heritage which was promised to his grandfather Abraham, as God swore to Isaac:

> I will perform the oath which I sware unto Abraham thy father; and I will make thy seed to multiply as the stars of heaven, and will give unto thy seed all these countries; and in thy seed shall all the nations of the earth be blessed; Because that Abraham obeyed my voice, and kept my charge, my commandments, my statues, and my laws (Gen. 26:3-5).

And now Jacob has the burden and blessing of this magnificent promise. With one eye on the world; with a secondhand faith—which he puts on and off like a coat, Jacob surely cannot expect the promise to work.

But I have some of the same feelings as I look at my own life, your life, and the life of any church member. There are too many Jacobs in the church, two many Jacobs serving as deacons, teachers in the Sunday School, and staff members. We carry the name and the heritage, yet there so often seems to be no difference from the world. No deeper relation to

God, no deeper values, no sacrificial commitment to our Lord and His church. How is God's will going to be done through these Jacobs?

Before Jacob can really mean anything to the kingdom of God, he must have his life radically changed! Just carrying the family name won't accomplish the purpose! So, are we saying we need a spiritual shot in the arm for John Doe—good ole boy, patriotic American? You mean a little flag waving and head bowing? No, I mean much more—watch the second act in this drama of our family album.

Jacob on the Run

He thought he had run clear past next Sunday before he even slowed down. Surely he was out of the reach of the God of his father and his grandfather. Such were Jacob's thoughts on the evening of that first day as an exile, as he fled his brother's wrath and his father's sorrow:

> I fled Him, down the nights and down the days;
> I fled Him down the arches of the years;
> I fled Him down the labyrinthine ways
> Of my own mind; and in the midst of tears
> I hid from Him, and under running laughter.
> Up vistaed hopes I sped;
> And shot, precipitated,
> Adown titanic glooms of chasmed fears,
> From those strong Feet that followed, followed after.
> ....
> Halts by me that footfall:
> Is my gloom, after all,
> Shade of His hand, outstretched caressingly?
> "Ah, fondest, blindest, weakest,
> I am He Whom thou seekest!

Thou dravest love from thee, who dravest Me."

Try to imagine the scene as he eats a sorry supper and lies down to sleep that night in a strange place we call Bethel. If you have ever been to the Holy Land and visited the area of Bethel, you can appreciate the words of the hymn:

> Though like the wanderer,
> The sun gone down,
> Darkness be over me,
> My rest a stone;
> Yet in my dreams I'd be
> Nearer, my God, to Thee.
>
> —Sarah F. Adams

Lonely, guilty, tired, surrounded by a darkness broken only by the glitter of the stars above, poor Jacob, mother's favorite and never the outdoor type, begins to think about God and the future. He huddles near a stone cliff, pulls a rock over for a pillow, and sleeps fitfully.

It is thought that our conscious minds are but the tip of the iceberg, and that our unconscious minds are where so much of the action takes place, and that at night! So it is with Jacob as he dreams. That dream is described in Genesis 28:12-16.

> And he dreamed, and behold a ladder set up on the earth, and the top of it reached to heaven: and behold the angels of God ascending and descending on it. And, behold, the Lord stood above it, and said, I am the Lord God of Abraham thy father, and the God of Isaac: the land whereon thou liest, to thee will I give it, and to thy seed; and thy seed shall be as the dust of

the earth, and thou shalt spread abroad to the west, and to the east, and to the north, and to the south: and in thee and in thy seed shall all the families of the earth be blessed. And, behold, I am with thee, and will keep thee in all places whither thou goest, and will bring thee again into this land; for I will not leave thee, until I have done that which I have spoken to thee of. And Jacob awaked out of his sleep, and he said, surely the Lord is in this place; and I knew it not.

It is obvious that Jacob's dream is more than he deserves; more beauty, more mercy. But what is the meaning of Jacob's dream? I feel that his dream means three things which every person who is running from God needs to understand and experience: first, deep down, in his subconscious mind and heart, *Jacob wanted a closer walk with God.* Nobody really intends to go it alone all the way. Second, *God was impressing His claim and His promise on Jacob.* God does that, you know. Of course, we can take our dreams and our inner impressions too seriously, but don't rule out the reality of God speaking to you through many different ways. And, third, Jacob realized, deep down, that *he could only reach the top of God's ladder by serving God.* But, like most of us, he did not walk a straight line immediately after this emotional experience.

Suddenly he snapped awake, eyes and ears straining, listening—was somebody out there? Only the shadow of a mighty rock; the gleaming stars overhead; the night sounds of the plaintive cry of the hunted, and an awesome presence. His heart was filled with fear and dread, and he knew—somehow, in his heart, he knew—"God is in this place, and I knew it not! How dreadful [full of majesty and worthy of awe] is this place! this is none other but the house of God, and this is the gate of heaven" (vv. 16-17).

When the First Touch Doesn't Take

He was right about that—this experience was the gate of heaven. But, with the rising sun dreams lose much of their power, and daylight helps to soothe troubled hearts. In the morning Jacob set up a pillar, poured oil on it to pacify the God he had not escaped, and made a bargain with God.

We want to put that bargain in it kindest light, yet we must be honest with the record—what a scoundrel! Trying to strike a bargain with God: "If you will take care of me and get me back home in one piece, I will acknowledge you and give a tithe." God didn't answer.

This experience shook Jacob and scared him, but it does not seem to have changed him. There was no basic change in the old Jacob. Is this where so many churchgoers are? Do we hear the promises in Christ, have an emotional experience in the stadium or church house, and then drift away when the dream fades? Do we have a crisis in our lives—illness, lose our job or our spouse—get scared and promise to rearrange the priorities in our lives, then when we can see daylight again, the fervent promises melt like the dew before the sun?

And so Jacob journeyed on through life. By then he was where many of us are this very day. As he journeyed, he met other clever men, shysters like himself, men of the world—like his uncle, Laban. Jacob went to live with Laban and his family, and fell in love with the beautiful Rachel, the younger daughter of Laban. Smitten with love, Jacob agreed to work seven years for Rachel, and they seemed like so many days, for the love he had for her.

But talk about a trickster—Laban threw one more wedding! The bridal gown trailed into the next county, and the veil was so heavy Jacob never got a glimpse of his beloved's face that night. Next morning, Jacob was speechless to find he had not married Rachel, but her older sister! We aren't told what Rachel thought about all this! An agreement was reached—seven more years as a hired hand—and Rachel was delivered to him in advance.

You know the story of how Jacob won in the end. He managed to get the old man's daughters—both of them—plus the livestock, and even Laban's household goods. After twenty years of outwitting his uncle, Jacob was ready to clear out with his booty. He turned homeward, feeling that surely things had quieted down, perhaps he would be welcomed back.

When, If Ever, Will a Man Change?

This going-home scene is one of the famous word pictures of the Bible. Jacob, ever a conniver, sent ahead to Esau, but the messengers were soon back with disturbing news—Esau was on the way with a force of 400 men! Jacob divided his family into two groups, so if one party was lost, perhaps some would be saved. The prayer in chapter 32:9-11, was the same old Jacob we have become familiar with. Then he prepared a present, sent the wives on over the ford Jabbok, and spent a sleepless night thinking about the encounter on the morrow.

So far, Jacob's life had revolved around romance, money, and getting ahead. His character and life were as spotted and "ringstreaked" as his cattle. His rationale for the presents to his brother sounded suspiciously like an effort to "pull the wool over his eyes" before he sees his face! Religion had not been decisive in his life, but now he came to the second night encounter with God Almighty.

Jacob was middleaged. When, if ever, was he going to change? When was he going to turn to God, live for God? Not until something happened that changed him inside! And, that night, something happened.

Verse 24 of chapter 32 puts it succinctly: "And Jacob was left alone; and there wrestled a man with him until the breaking of the day." It was a wrestling match of some sort—in his mind? Physically? What does it mean? Was it another dream? I think he actually wrestled with a physical being, and no doubt at first when this intruder in the night seized him, he must have thought his brother Esau had attacked! Looking at it afterward, Jacob felt he had wrestled with the angel of God.

What did it mean? All his life was summed up that night: all his life he had been fighting God, and finally he realized he could never win. He saw he must accept God's will for his life. In that time of mighty struggle, Jacob became desperate for the presence and power of God: "I will not let thee go, except thou bless me" (v. 26). That was formerly his attitude toward the world! There was no bargaining this time; only the fierce clinging of a little man to a bigger opponent.

That meeting, finally, made a permanent mark on Jacob's life. Whatever else happened that night in his anxiety, fear, guilt, danger—the point is that he wrestled with God until he became God's man, and he gained peace and help. His name changed from Jacob, "the supplanter," to Israel, "prince of God." His character changed: he developed a new outlook on himself and on his possessions. Somehow the blessing is often more easily sought and more easily received in the darkness.

Perhaps the most beautiful scene in the story, and most certainly Jacob's finest hour, was the next morning "And as he passed over Penuel the sun rose upon him, and he halted [limped] upon his thigh" (v. 31). Time fails us to speak fully of the marvelous and powerful spiritual truth that wounded souls are God's choice people. Sometimes we have to be given a limp to bring us to God, to help us see our frailty. But so often it is one of God's choicest vessels who limps, however invisible it may be. There has probably never been a Southern Baptist, or any other kind, of pastor so powerfully used of God as George W. Truett. Let me tell you of his limp.

A former Texas Ranger had become the police chief of Dallas and was a fine member of the First Baptist Church. He loved his new pastor, George Truett, and invited him to go quail hunting. Late in the afternoon, coming out of the fields, Captain Arnold was walking a few yards in front of Truett, and as Truett shifted his gun from one arm to the other, it fired. The wound, in the calf of the Arnold's leg, was not felt to be serious by anyone but Truett. Almost instantly he was filled with a premonition that it would be fatal. And his worse fears came true as the Captain died within a few hours. Truett felt he could never preach again, that he would have to leave the ministry. As the weekend approached, he faced the question of whether he could or should enter the pulpit again. Late Saturday night he continued to pace and to pray. Finally, deciding to try to preach, he went to bed and slept for the first time since the accident.

During the night there came a dream to him in which he saw Jesus, as vividly as some earthly friend, standing beside him. The Master said, "Do not be afraid. You are my man from now on." This dream came not once, but three times.

The dream was a turning point in the life of George Truett. From then on he had no doubts as to the reality of Jesus and of his commission as Christ's man. And hear the comments of a church member concerning that first Sunday back in the pulpit: "But his voice! I shall never forget his voice that morning, as we heard for the first time that note of sadness and pathos which now we know so well. It seemed to carry the burden of all the grief in the world."[1]

The last scene in the life of Jacob, or Israel, is found in the forty-eighth chapter of Genesis, as he lies dying in the land of Egypt. Listen to the man who used to be the rogue Jacob:

> God, before whom my fathers Abraham and Isaac did walk, the God which fed me all my life long until this day, The Angel which redeemed me from all evil, bless the lads; and let my name be named on them, and the name of my fathers Abraham and Isaac; and let them grow into a multitude in the midst of the earth (vv. 15-16).

The most valuable possession Jacob had to give at the end of his life was his relationship to God! He confessed God's hand had fed him, God had redeemed and guided him, and his prayer was that God's will would be done in his family's life.

How mysteriously God does work! Here at the end, it is as at the beginning—a laying on of hands, the giving of a blessing! How Jacob would love that old hymn:

> Nearer, my God, to Thee,
> Nearer to Thee!
> E'en though it be a cross
> That raiseth me;
> Still all my song shall be,
> Nearer, my God, to Thee.

Where are you in your journey through life? Like Jacob at Bethel, troubled in heart and soul? Like Jacob wrestling with the angel of God, seeking the light? God grant you to see the cross on which Jesus died for every Jacob, even you.

17
What Goes Up Doesn't Have to Come Down
Luke 19:1-10

Zaccheus, make haste, and come down; for today I must abide at thy house (Luke 9:5).

Ever since Isaac Newton watched that apple fall in his garden some three hundred years ago, we have known that what goes up must come down! It is an unbreakable law; it holds true for rockets and rocks, for baseballs and balloons.

But in the spiritual realm this is not the case. In the New Testament is an interesting story about a man who went *up,* but that same man didn't come *down.* Luke 19 records one man's spiritual pilgrimage—yet it is instructive for us all.

Let's break the story of Zaccheus into four parts—the better to store it in our minds. There is, first of all, the *man who went up* into the tree. Second, there is *what happened up there,* followed by the *man who came down,* and last, there is the fascinating matter of *what happened down there.*

The Man Who Went Up Into the Tree

Physically this man looked, I suppose, like a thousand other men of Israel. But Luke takes pains to describe him in several ways. "Which was the chief among the publicans" (v. 2*a*). He was a tax collector. Now we are all familiar with tax collectors, and, in general, they are not a bad lot. In fact, they even have to run for office in most areas of this nation. That was not the case in Galilee of the first century.

Tax collecting was a job farmed out on a commission basis. You collected all you could, then paid Rome, and pocketed the rest—and Rome asked very few questions. The temptation was great; most tax collectors were scandal-ridden. They paid a high price for their wealth; these "publicans" or tax farmers were considered, along with thieves, as especially unclean. They were often actually considered thieves or robbers.

Not only was our man Zaccheus a tax collector; he was the *chief* publican. This may mean he had purchased the tax-collecting rights for the Jericho area and had several underling collectors working for him.

"And he was rich" (v. 2*b*). Hated—but rich! Notice how the word "rich" was flung at him, as if it were both a despicable and exactly right word by which to describe him. I have often wondered how you and I would fare if people had to choose just one word by which to sum us up! Would they say: ". . . and he was *honest;* . . . she was a *gossip;* . . . he was *jolly;* . . . he was a *sad face*"

Probably two other features capture the essence of Zaccheus. He no doubt wore the latest fashions, and he was a short fellow. And I imagine that business of being called "Shorty" rankled, too.

By the way, that's what brought him to the sycamore tree—his short stature.

On this particular day, the man called Jesus is to come by this way. Zaccheus has heard of Jesus, and is naturally curious about the man and the fuss that is raised about Him. And that's how this short, little man came to be up a tree.

Now, any difference between Zaccheus and all other unsaved persons is completely superficial. Here's the *real* man who climbed up that tree: a once-born, ego-centered, sinful fellow. Zaccheus is living in his own strength, like most folks. His priorities are all fouled up; he's speeding down a dead-end road, traveling as fast as he can go.

He would fit well in America during these days of civil religion. He no doubt loves to call on God—to do Zaccheus' bidding. He probably thinks God agrees with him on everything. He may enjoy a savage kind of delight in his outcast situation, inwardly feeling quite righteous at the synagogue services, although he knows people are talking behind his back. He lets God make all the big decisions in his life—there simply haven't been any of those in a long time, so Zaccheus takes care of the little decisions (so as not to bother God with such, you know).

Zaccheus *knows,* but does not *believe,* that his life is a farce spiritually. He is familiar with the trappings of religion. Today as he strolls down the narrow streets of Jericho he has not faced up to his own self-love and evil.

Zaccheus has heard of Jesus, although he has never met Him. He has not seen or known the Stranger of Galilee, but there is a hunger in his soul to meet Him. In this, too, he is like every unsaved person. For God has so made us, as Augustine wrote, to have a hunger for Him, and we are restless until we rest in Him. Zaccheus probably does not know why he decided on this route to the office this morning, a route which crosses the Galilean's path. He is like a blind man groping at a wall, looking for a door—because a door *should* be there, *ought* to be there.

In such a frame of mind he hears the sounds of a crowd

coming his way. Still a block or two away, there is time to seek a good vantage point from which to survey the crowd and to study this man. So a stout sycamore tree with limbs close to the ground caught his attention. True, it was a bit undignified to be climbing trees at his age, but then no one would see him clamber up, no one would notice him up in the tree, and he could come down at his leisure after the crowd had passed. Only a brief, undignified moment and he is on his perch.

What Happened Up There

And now he sits, partly camouflaged behind the limbs and leaves. I think three words could describe Zacchaeus at this point: *scornful, amused,* and *searching.* He is scornful of the dirty crowd—not that he would come right out and say that, of course. But it was true that the Carpenter seemed to gather the riffraff; his crowds normally were not made up of clean, respectable, scholarly types or students or wealthy laymen like the Pharisees.

To be sure, among the crowd there are scribes and Pharisees, as Zaccheus could see, but he knows these fellows are part of the accreditation committee sent out from the headquarters. Then there are the innocent-looking folks, probably Galileans, and the curious—who we always have with us—who follow to see the odd cures people claimed Jesus could do. There are the beggars and aged, who tag along for lack of better to do or to get a handout.

The crowd has now come into sight and is moving closer to the sycamore tree. It is now almost directly in front of Zaccheus. Intent upon scanning the crowd, *the old Zaccheus* who clambered up into that tree does not realize that he has only a few more seconds of existence! And then it happens. The Scripture simply describes what happens like this: "And when Jesus came to the place, he looked up, and saw him, and said unto him, Zaccheus, make haste, and come down; for today I must abide at thy house."

It is enough to make a new man out of Zaccheus! Do you suppose there was a background we have not mentioned, a prior meeting unrecorded in the New Testament? We cannot say, and be that as God wills, here we see a stubborn will melt as he looks into the eyes of the Master. We do know that Zaccheus's spiritual need is so great—yes, and so near to bursting, perhaps so ripe—that this one gesture on Jesus' part speaks volumes. "Come on down, Zaccheus, I'm planning to have dinner at your house!"

As we consider what happened up that tree, let us mark that in every life *there must be a confrontation* of our rebellious hearts with God's love. A confrontation now—or later. The Holy Spirit desires to deal with the sin in our lives.

In each life there are situations full of the presence of the seeking Savior. You could meet Him on some such unnamed road, or in some common pew. My favorite illustration of how God speaks to our spiritual need in the common experiences of life is the true story of the man who, after attending church for years, finally came forward and made his profession of faith. After the service the minister, feeling sure it was his super preaching which led to this conversion, asked the man just what point or statement led to his seeing his need for Christ. "Well," replied the man, "what really spoke to me was your statement that you had finished the first half of your sermon, and it was time to go on to the second part. I suddenly realized that it was time for me to be finished with the first part of my life, and go on to the second part, the commitment to Christ!"

No two experiences with Jesus are exactly alike. I've never known another man who was converted while up in a tree, as Zaccheus was! I was converted in a proasic way, in a typical Southern Baptist church, while giving only half-attention to what was, to an eleven-year-old boy, a rather boring sermon. But no other person was ever converted exactly like I was. You may have come to Jesus in the aftermath of some heartrending tragedy, or may have been converted while walking down some sandy country lane, the sand squishing between your toes. Each of us has his own story of conversion with its own special character. I can hear Zaccheus as he gives his testimony: ". . . and there I sat, up in that tree . . ."

What Kind of Man Came Down from the Tree

"And he made haste, and came down, and received him joyfully" (v. 6). Zaccheus is a beautiful testimony to the change Paul says takes place in conversion: "Therefore if any man be in Christ, he is a new creature: old things are passed away; behold, all things are become new" (2 Cor. 5:17).

Do any of you remember the locust hulls you used to collect as a boy? Perhaps I should also say, remember the locust hulls the boys used to tease you with when you were a little girl! I saw one the other day, clinging to the side of a tree. An empty sleeve of an insect, every part of every leg sculptured yet hollow, with a big split down the back of the hull. He's gone! That's the way it was with Zaccheus. If we had been there, and had been able to see the invisible, maybe we would have seen the hull of the old Zaccheus still sitting there, lifelike but empty and dead. For Zaccheus became a new creation in Christ!

And, just as there were only superficial differences between the old Zaccheus and other sinners, so now the *similarities* between the old and new Zaccheus are only surface in their depth. He still looks like the old man. He wears the same suit, but he's a new man.

He is full of a newfound *joy*. "And he made haste, and came down, and received him joyfully." This new joy Christ brings with Him is not just a bubbly sort of happiness; its chief character is rather that of a spring welling up within the Christian, which draws others who are thirsting for the eternal water.

Zacchaeus is eager for a *closer walk*. He is not concerned over whether the house is clean, or whether the wife knows Jesus is coming for dinner—the glory of walking with the Master overshadows all! He has already wasted enough years and wants to make his life count! He seems oblivious to the criticism of the crowd, as is Jesus: "And when they saw it, they all murmured, saying, That he was gone to be guest with a man that is a sinner" (v. 7). Like the disciples at the Transfiguration, "seeing Jesus only," Zaccheus is anxious to obey whatever he perceives is Jesus' will.

Zacchaeus brings with him from the tree a *new set of priorities*. And that leads us to look at the fourth segment of our story.

What Happened Down There

What happened was that this man, a new babe in Christ, proceeded to demonstrate his new life in Christ. Listen to what he said within minutes of his spiritual birth: "And

Zaccheus stood, and said unto the Lord; behold, Lord, the half of my goods I give to the poor; and if I have taken any thing from any man by false accusation, I restore him fourfold" (v. 8).

One half to the poor! Four times back to anyone he had robbed! How those sinners in the Bible did *demonstrate* their conversion! Zaccheus gives away a fortune! Simply put, *an inner change found outer expression.*

A genuine conversion experience demands some testimony, some expression of its depth and reality, beginning with a public commitment as soon as possible. Somewhere I read about a man of meager education and means who was ministered to and led to the Lord by a neighborhood church. He overflowed with the joy of his salvation and the fellowship of his new friends. One night he confided to his wife that he wanted so badly to be a part of the church softball team, but had no jersey with writing on it like the other men. His dear wife could read no better than he, but she determined to sew him a jersey and put some writing on it, so he would be as properly outfitted as the other men. As she sewed one day, she saw a bright new sign being put in the window of a grocery across the street. The writing on the sign looked good to her, although she hadn't the faintest idea what it said. So she sewed the same letters onto her husband's jersey, and proudly presented it to him. And he wore it just as proudly to play the next game with his church ball team. And nobody laughed, for they all knew that he was indeed "Under New Management" since giving his heart to Jesus!

How well I remember one man who responded at the close of the service in the little church my wife and I attended for awhile during seminary days. He was the owner of a liquor store, and made a vow that he would put an axe to the store's stock the following morning. I rose early and turned up with quite a crowd of other members to see him carry out his vow. Of course, the main reason was to give support and encouragement to him in his new walk with the Lord—but as the one who had preached the night before, I was awed at the way God used the message and just wanted to see this sinner use the axe!

How different his life would have been if Zaccheus had slouched down in the leaves of the sycamore tree that day and ignored the gentle invitation of Jesus—if he had stared back, stone-faced, and then, when the curious crowd had finished peering up into the tree and passed by, had stumbled down and wandered off into his spiritual darkness. How tragic is the very thought!

Yet that is a danger you may be facing right now. For, you see, Jesus passes by even in this message. Right by your sycamore tree. I beg of you, hear His gentle voice calling to you: "John . . . Mary . . . Bill . . . Sue . . . make haste, and come down; for today I must have dinner at your house." Don't hide and then stumble on off into spiritual darkness.

18
Heaven's Gates
Revelation 21:10-13,21,25

On the east three gates; on the north three gates; on the south three gates; and on the west three gates (Rev. 21:13).

One of the radiant visions of the Revelation is this scene of the Holy City descending out of heaven, having the glory of God. The writer pictures a walled city with three gates on each side. Three gates on the north, three on the east, three on the west, and three on the south. By each gate stood an angel, and on the gates were written the names of the twelve tribes of Israel.

Our description of the "pearly gates" of heaven are taken from these verses, along with the golden streets of our favorite gospel songs. The gates are never closed, for there is no night there.

Anyone who has visited the earthly Jerusalem and gazed at its walls and gates from the Mount of Olives has a vivid picture of what the writer had in mind. Every time I read these verses a bit of poetry comes to mind:

> Heaven's gates were open wide,
> But still the gypsies camped outside.[1]

Gypsies: Physical and Spiritual

The tragedy lies in the second line: "But still the gypsies camped outside." The older among us remember the gypsy bands which used to roam our highways. We have seen the camps just outside the city limits, and as kids we stared at the crystal balls these strange people carried and at the dangling earrings and bandannas they wore. They would camp right outside the city, avoiding the responsibilities of citizenship of the town, yet enjoying the benefits; they avoided involvement, yet gained privileges.

We still have gypsies, only now we call them hoboes, tramps, transients. They turn up at my church and yours both day and night, asking for a handout to help them reach the next time.

They may not look like the old-time gypsies but they are gypsies all the same. They don't want to be domesticated, to settle down, to accept the responsibilities of citizenship. Such folks are pathetic, and it is doubly so when children are involved. Both adults and children look pinched in their faces, weary of eye and hand, marked by the beast of time.

Now let me speak to you of spiritual gypsies. These are a pathetic group, too. They do not bear the marks of these *physical* gypsies—they are clean and perfumed, often wear the latest fashions, and usually are larded over with beauty treatments to escape the mark of time.

They wander in their finery from church to church, not asking for a handout, but never *giving* themselves fully to any fellowship. Always finding something wrong with the church they are visiting, they pull up spiritual stakes, pack up spiritual tents, and move on to the next church. Bound by their sins, ignorant of God's peace, lacking the fullness of the fellowship of the church, like ships in the night, they pass on. I am sure I do not exaggerate when I say that in any congregation on any given Sunday there are spiritual gypsies in the crowd—folks who have a clear spiritual kinship with Nicodemus who, until the end, camped barely outside the pale of discipleship; with the multitudes who followed Jesus —but at a distance, never committing their hearts to Him; like the rich young ruler, who was unwilling to pay the price to enter the Holy City:

> Heaven's gates were open wide;
> Still the gypsies camped outside.

Why Do the Gypsies Camp Outside?

I've asked physical gypsies over and over that question —and often they really don't know! But spiritual gypsies seem to camp outside for two major reasons. First is a *tragic understanding of God's claim,* which they reject. I wish I had a dollar for every person who has said to me concerning the new walk the gospel requires—"I can never live up to that standard!" These spiritual gypsies so often seem to hear the Word of God's demand upon our lives more clearly than many church members. "Ye cannot serve God and mammon!" And they are unwilling to give up the love of the world, even though they know their uncommitted lives are wrong. They will often count the cost and decide that to follow Jesus in a serious, discipleship way is beyond either their desire or ability to achieve. They are the pearl merchant who, seeing the pearl of great price, decides it is *not* worth all one has!

How hard it is to get past the specter of the young man to whom Jesus said: "Go . . . sell . . . give . . . come . . . follow me . . ." I would to God our church members had more understanding of the *demand of God's grace,* and that the spiritual gypsies had more grasp of the *grace of God's demand!*

The second major reason that spiritual gypsies camp outside the Holy City is a *tragic misunderstanding of God's will.* So many folks feel that "if I surrender my life to God, if I open my life to His lordship, if I step through the gates, He'll take away the joy of my life, He'll make me a pale shadow of the kind of happy person I want to be. What a rebuke this is to the kind of testimony we Christians give to the world! We have communicated to those outside the realm of grace that our God is a cold, sad, vengeful God who takes away the joy, the perfume of life!

Yet the Bible says the person who enters the gates of new life in Christ is saved from the wrath of God. That person is made an heir of God; he is filled with joy, peace, and forgiveness. Jesus declared He came that we might have life, and have it more abundantly; that is, drink of joy even more deeply!

The Open Gate

Before every spiritual gypsy there stands this hour three great truths: *the open gate, the reality of people who pass by, and the tragic consequences of ignoring the open gate.* Consider with me these statements which may change your life.

The gates of heaven will one day close—for you. Those gates which are always open in heaven will be closed one day here. They will most certainly be closed when the Lord returns, and time shall be no more, and the trumpet shall summon all people to judgment. And that day could be today. In any case, the gates will most certainly close here on earth for you when death overtakes the gypsy on some dark and lonely road.

Those gates are surely closed when the heart of the gypsy is so hardened that he fails to hear or to heed the gentle calling of the Holy Spirit. As we are told in the Epistle to the Hebrews: "But exhort one another daily, while it is called To-day; lest any of you be hardened through the deceitfulness of sin. . . . To-day if ye will hear his voice, harden not your hearts, as in the provocation. So we see that they could not enter in because of unbelief" (3:13, 15, 19).

Little wonder preachers through the ages have pleaded with the gypsies to enter the gates of life before it is too late. In one of his sermons Charles Haddon Spurgeon powerfully stressed the danger looming before the gypsy by describing his own funeral:

"In a little while,' he said, 'there will be a concourse of persons in the streets. Methinks I hear someone enquiring:

"What are all these people waiting for?"

"Do you not know? He is to be buried today."

"And who is that?"

"It is Spurgeon."

"What—the man that preached at the Tabernacle?"

"Yes, he is to be buried today."

"That will happen very soon. And when you see my coffin carried to the silent grave, I should like every one of you, whether converted or not, to be constrained to say, 'He did earnestly urge us, in plain and simple language, not to put off the consideration of eternal things; he did entreat us to look to Christ. Now he is gone, our blood is not at his door if we perish.' "[2]

> Heaven's gates were open wide;
> Still the gypsies camped outside.

What a frightful caravan these spiritual gypsies form as they pass time after time by the open gates of heaven. Fully planning, clearly intending in their hearts one day to enter the gates of new life. If only people could feel the urgency in the stories Jesus told of those who move through life with an attitude that the gates will always be open!

In Matthew 25 Jesus describes what should have been a happy occasion, a wedding feast, but instead was turned into a time of sadness because some of the bridesmaids presumed on the kindness of the bridegroom. "Afterward came also the other virgins, saying, Lord, Lord, open to us. But he answered and said, Verily I say unto you, I know you not" (Matt. 25:11-12).

> Heaven's gates were open wide;
> Still the gypsies camped outside.

Almost But Not Quite

There are some in every congregation of whom it could be said as Jesus said to the scribe: "Thou art not far from the kingdom of God" (Mark 12:34). *That is the tragic story of the gypsies—almost, but not quite.*

I remember going to an auction years ago when my children were very young. It was pretty dull until the auctioneer held up an old, beat-up, little child's chair which had once been painted white. Its wicker seat was much the worse for wear, but my little daughter fell in love with it. I doubt it was worth more than five dollars—if that much—at the time. But how can a father refuse the wistful look in the big brown eyes of his only daughter?

Someone else—I never knew who—over on the other side of the crowd must have had a little daughter in love with the same chair! The bidding kept climbing. If I said ten, he said twelve; if I said twenty, he said twenty-two fifty. And so, I finally gave the battle up, and some man bought a most expensive child's chair. For some time I lived with the reproach that I had almost fulfilled my daughter's dream—but not quite. I almost got the chair, but that was not enough!

A pilot calls upon all his skills to bring the crippled aircraft in for a landing. He nurses it into the landing pattern; he can see the runway now, beckoning to him. The trees are flashing by below, closer and closer; the end of the asphalt ribbon seems so close, just a little more power out of the crippled engines, and he will make it. And he almost does. Not quite, but almost! And over one hundred passengers died.

The telephone rings, perhaps late at night, and the voice is broken, full of tears. A husband has just been tragically killed; could the minister come over and talk with the wife and children? He goes, and gives what comfort he can, not knowing the family. He asks some questions: "Was your husband a Christian? Did he know Jesus as Lord and Savior?" And the reply is soft, yearning, and uncertain: "He was a good man . . . he loved his wife and children. He was active in his civic club . . . well-liked around town. He was a good provider. I really don't know if he was a Christian, but he was a good man."

Almost a Christian—but not quite. And a miss is as good as a mile!

> Heaven's gates were open wide;
> Still the gypsies camped outside.

The Gypsies' Choice

The gates of heaven are still open wide for you, because you have been given this, another day, in which to decide what you will do with Jesus. But *not even God will make a man enter the gates of heaven.*

Living in a medical community I have noticed a frightening parallel between the efforts of the surgeons and the saving work of God. So often all the work of the dedicated surgeon is to no avail because the patient's body rejects the transplant of the organ. That which could bring about health and happiness is rejected by the body itself in a twisted and tragic form of suicide!

Time after time I have seen men and women, boys and girls under conviction of sin by the Holy Spirit, yet they reject "so great salvation"—rejecting the only thing which can bring happiness and fulfillment to their lives, marching right by the open gates!

> The gates of heaven are open wide;
> *Let's us gypsies go inside!*

19
The Heartbreak of Backsliding
John 6:66-71

From that time many of his disciples went back, and walked no more with him (John 6:66).

In one of those books your grandmother read by lamplight, your mother read as part of the English course in high school, and you may not have read at all, *The Pilgrim's Progress,* John Bunyan describes the backsliding Christian. His hero, Christian, is on pilgrimage to the Celestial City and is talking along the journey with another pilgrim named Hopeful. The conversation turns to a man known to both, named Temporary, who lived in the village of Graceless, next door to a man called Turnback. Temporary had once declared his intention of going with these men on the pilgrimage, but fell by the wayside.

In their conversation, Hopeful gives four reasons Temporary backslid: his conscience was awakened, but his mind was not changed; slavish fears "overmastered" him; he became ashamed of his religion; and, he disliked to experience guilt or meditate on judgment.

The Pilgrim's Definition of Backsliding

Hopeful then asks Christian to explain the manner of the backsliding of Temporary and folks of his kind, which

Christian does, making a sort of list: (1) they turn their thoughts as much as possible from God, death, and judgment to come; (2) next they lose interest in private devotions, the curbing of lusts, sorrow for sin, etc.; (3) then they spurn the company of the committed; (4) after that, they grow cold to public worship and Bible study; (5) then they begin to "pick holes, as we say, in the coats of some of the godly" in order to run down religion; (6) then they begin to run with carnal, loose, and wanton folks; (7) they then give way to carnal discourses in secret; (8) after this they "begin to play with little sins openly"; (9) and then, "being thus hardened, they show themselves as they are."

Sound familiar? There's not much I could add to this over three-hundred-year-old definition of backsliding and its manner. Bunyan would feel right at home observing most Baptist churches today, with nearly one-third of our members unaccounted for!

Bunyan popularized the term "backsliding" and it became a stock phrase among the frontier denominations of Baptists, Methodists, and Presbyterians. In our time the term may be a bit vague, so in preparation for preaching on the topic of backsliding, I asked my church staff for their understanding of the term. One CB buff put it both colorfully and succinctly: "A backslider is a Christian with his ears off . . . his antenna down." Right on! And to dress it up a little: "a backslider is a Christian whose love and commitment has grown cold."

Backsliding: New Testament Variety

The text story illumines the meaning of backsliding. The crowds had been following Jesus, and then in the sixth chapter of John He delivers some "hard statements," words with which the crowd did not agree, or did not understand, or both. And Jesus finds they don't really care; they turn and leave—to find a smaller messiah. Then follows a pathetic scene as the Master turns to The Twelve and asks if they, too, are going to desert Him. And that says to me powerfully that backsliding is a real possibility in the life of every Christian. Not a single one of us is above the temptation of letting our love for Christ grow cold. Nor are entire churches free from this possibility, as the admonition to the church at Ephesus in Revelation reveals.

The Bible does not hide the reality of this sin of backsliding. In the parable of the sower we recognize this sin in the seed which falls on rocky soil and quickly springs up, only to fall away. "And these are they likewise which are sown on stony ground; who, when they have heard the word, immediately receive it with gladness; And have no root in themselves, and so endure for a time: afterward, when affiction or persecution ariseth for the world's sake, immediately they are offended" (Mark 4:16-17). And in the same parable we are warned of the choking effects of the cares of this world and the deceitfulness of riches. "And these are they which are sown among thorns; such as hear the word, And the cares of this world, and the deceitfulness of riches, and the lusts of other things entering in, choke the word, and it becomes unfruitful" (vv. 18-19). The melancholy scene of Peter denying Christ should be proof aplenty of the nearness of this sin. And Paul writes to the Galatians who have fallen away in the persuasion of the Judaizers: "Ye did run well; who did hinder you?" (5:7).

Backsliding Baptists

Backsliding is not just a biblical problem; the modern church, as I earlier indicated, is riddled with such folks. A few months ago I visited an earlier pastorate, and was thumbing through the church pictorial directory lying on the coffee table in the home where I was a guest. The conversation turned to a similar directory made years before when I was pastor. The family had one, and so we spent a delightful time chuckling over what the years had done to all of us. But, time and again, as I remarked that such-and-such a family was so active in my time there, my host would ponder and say, "You know, I haven't seen them in a long time." Or, "Yes, they used to be active, but . . ."

Listen, there is probably not a Baptist church in your city which could hold its members if they all decided to come to church on the same Sunday! We don't count on faithfulness out of our members. We build in expectations of unfaithfulness and backsliding! There can be no argument about the reality of backsliding, both in the Bible and in the modern church.

The Effect of Our Backsliding

Backsliding has a fatal effect, first of all, on you as an individual Christian. When you cease to be fervent for the Lord, when you cease to be active in the work of your church, when you cease your spiritual life of prayer and devotions, when you cease to support the work of your church with your tithe—you forfeit the *joy of your salvation*. We would do well to remember David's anguished plea to the Lord after his sin with Bathsheba. He had grown cold toward the Lord, and made his cry: "Restore unto me the joy of thy salvation" (Ps. 51:12). Our churches are stuffed with members who are stuffed with the things of the world and starving for a real relationship with God.

Every Sunday I have the privilege of preaching to tens of thousands of folks by television, and I am aware that some of these people are backslidden church members who ought to be in their churches worshiping the Lord with their fellow church members. But somewhere along the way their hearts grew cold and indifferent—it matters not *why;* the terrible spiritual cost is too much to pay, whatever the reason.

The old story is so fitting about the church's new minister who went visiting a backslidden church member. The man had not darkened the church door in years. They both sat before the open fire for awhile, just staring into the flames. Finally the minister took the fire tongs, and, reaching over, grasped a flaming coal with the tongs and rolled it away from the other logs. They both sat in silence while the coal, apart from the others, slowly turned from red-hot to a faint glow and then to a cold, black cinder. Then the backslidden man turned to the minister with tears in his eyes and said, "I'll be there Sunday, Preacher."

We lose meaningful fellowship in the faith when we backslide, but we lose even more—we *lose the partnership in the gospel.* Paul spoke of that partnership so effectively in his letter to the church at Philippi, thanking God "For your fellowship in the gospel from the first day until now" (1:5). The backslider can have no genuine feeling of partnership in the gospel with his pastor, his fellow church members, or his denomination's missionary outreach. Long years ago in one of my earliest pastorates, I knew a man who had stopped going to church because a girl joined the church one Sunday morning, and then partook of the Lord's Supper that night before being baptized. This man, a deacon, stomped out of the church that night and, when I knew him, had not been back for over a decade. What a tragedy! A man became a backslider for over a decade over such a small matter! How the devil does his work!

Consider not only the effect of your backsliding on you as one member, but also *the effect of your backsliding on your church*. It means there is one less Christian to do the work of your church. It means the other members who are seeking to carry out the fellowship and mission of the church must carry your load. It means the rest of the church will have to spend time putting out the brush fires you will undoubtedly start with a critical tongue toward your pastor, your fellow members, and your church in general. And all because you are not right with God.

But even worse than hurting yourself, and hurting your church, *your backsliding will hurt the Lord*. Think again on the text picture and see the Lord saying with sadness in his voice: "Will ye also go away?" Must He find, throughout all the centuries, that even among those who respond, "Lord, to whom shall we go? Thou hast the words of eternal life" (vv. 67-68), that these also, for such small and petty reasons, will turn away, will backslide?

Why Christians Backslide

While we're looking into the mirror of our commitment, let's consider some of the causes of our backsliding. The first reason may well be *incomplete "conversions."* Too often there was no genuine conversion. That is the case in the text story, for Jesus tells the crowd "Ye seek me, not because ye saw the miracles, but because ye did eat of the loaves, and were filled" (v. 26). The people followed because of what they could get. They followed because they got all carried away with emotion—this was the latest sensation. And in our day, the mixture of cheap grace, gaudy sensationalism, and crowd approval results too often in a "conversion" which is not real. I think this is part of what the writer is saying in 1 John when we read: "They went out from us, *but they were not of us* [author's italics]; for if they had been of us, they would no doubt have continued with us." (2:19).

Yet another factor in our backsliding is often *some looming sin*. Obviously there are those in whose hearts God has done a work of grace, and yet they have apparently turned their backs upon Jesus and His church. I have clearly seen that in some cases the problem is a grievous slip into sin or some sinful aspect of life they have continued to cherish and nourish after conversion. And this sin, like a dreadful cancer, has continued to grow, and finally it has become so big it has overshadowed their relationship to God and the church. Like some awful sinkhole which opens up under a road or house, it keeps spreading while houses and cars tumble in.

If that is the case in your life, listen carefully. Is your sin *that* big? Is it really bigger than God's offer of forgiveness? Is it so big that all the love of your church is overpowered by it? No sin is that big! Jesus came to do battle with sin and evil and He has overcome the Evil One. Consider again your conversion experience and the days when you were on fire for the church and the Lord.

Another foothold the devil uses to promote backsliding

THE HEARTBREAK OF BACKSLIDING 197

is *some grievance against the church.* Some folks fall out with a fellow Christian, and the result is the withering of their spiritual life. Some folks get their feelings hurt by something the preacher says, or something he doesn't say, or because they don't agree on minors in the faith. The Bible lays down guidelines for dealing with grievances against any fellow church member, and we ought to follow them rather than be childish or foolish. It is a shame, but it may be that more backsliding results from imagined slights from church members than from genuinely tragic bouts with some huge sin.

Often no known sin, slight, or affront over being confronted with the clear teaching of Jesus is at the bottom of a backslidden life. *Sometimes we become backsliders simply in the living of these days.* Our spiritual bucket simply develops a leak, and much of our spiritual commitment leaks out.

There are some times and events in every life that need to be marked with a red flag—areas of high potential for spiritual backsliding. Young folks, red flag the college years. That's when you are out from under your parents' guiding eye, and the temptation is severe to drop out of church and let your spiritual life suffer. Let's red flag the early years of marriage. So often love *is* blind concerning the spiritual relationship of marriage. Are both you and your marriage partner Christians? Are you both of the same denomination? If you are on the way to the altar, have you carefully discussed this vital area of life and decided in which church you will plant your lives and your family?

Red flag the promotion years; the years when you begin to climb the corporate ladder of success. All of a sudden you will seem too busy for regular worship and church participation. Your tithe will begin to seem too big for your church;

after all, you think, *they don't wisely use what you already give.*

We sometimes put either a blue or pink bow on the mailbox or door when a baby is born—but often a red flag should be raised at this event! Children do not keep parents from church, but we often use them as excuses for backsliding. And, don't let the devil lull you with this one: "We'll get active in church when the children get older; we know they need to be in Sunday School." They surely do, and so do their parents!

The biggest red flag of all should be hoisted over the home in which more and more excuses are given for decreasing participation in church and a dwindling spiritual life. Start listening to yourself, and if your excuses are just that—excuses—if the ox seems always to be in the ditch, then either fill in the ditch or kill the ox! Excuses will cripple a spiritual life. The road to backsliding is paved with excuses.

Can a Backslider Come Back?

The reality of backsliding is obvious. *How can we backsliders come back to a closer walk with God?* Be sure to remember this: as a backslider, the distance you've put between God and yourself means nothing—the tragedy is not in the distance. The tragedy came in the first cooling of your love for the Savior.

Sometimes it seems to require a tragedy, an emergency, or crisis to bring a backslider back to God. I pray that such will not need to happen in your life. You can come back to God without that.

Jesus gave us, in His message to the church at Ephesus found in Revelation, three simple steps by which we backsliders can come back. *Remember.* Look in your life; evaluate your closeness to God and the church. There's not a Christian alive who doesn't remember his early days in the faith with warmth and joy. What happened? Once you become aware of the causes of your backslidden condition, the next step is clear. *Repent.* Turn around; don't go further away. Only explorers like Magellan ever get back where they started by going the other way! Turn your habits, your values around and come back to Christ. *Do the first works.* Start attending church. Start having your devotional time. Start witnessing for Christ. Let Christ be glorified in your life.

> O to grace how great a debtor
> Daily I'm constrained to be!
> Let Thy goodness, like a fetter,
> Bind my wand'ring heart to Thee:
> Prone to wander, Lord, I feel it,
> Prone to leave the God I love.
>
> —Robert Robinson

20
The Gospel of the Second Chance
John 8:1-11

Neither do I condemn thee: go, and sin no more (John 8:11).

Selling ladies' shoes is an education in itself. So you can see how I received two educations at once while in seminary! As a shoe salesman at one of the shopping malls in Raleigh, and then again in Louisville, I received an education in human vanity. I also learned some valuable lessons in human imperfections. And not the least lesson was the practical course in human gullibility!

I was reminded of my shoe store days by a recent Ann Landers column. A shoe salesman wrote in to say that a few days earlier he had waited on a woman whose husband was so jealous he didn't even want the salesman to touch her feet! So the husband had to go shopping with his wife each time she needed—or wanted—shoes, and fit her himself. The crux of the complaint of the shoe salesman was that the manager of the shoe store had denied him his commission on the sale because, said the manager, he didn't wait on the lady!

As I reflected on his letter and my own experiences in that noble profession, including the day I sold one dear lady twenty-four—that's right, count 'em, twenty-four—pairs of shoes, I came to see some of the lessons of shoe selling. In that face-to-face or rather face-to-feet kind of situation, many of the common and basic truths of life come alive.

Nobody's Perfect

For instance, selling shoes helped me to realize that not all feet are alike. I also learned *how* ladies buy shoes, and there's no denying it! Women buy shoes by the numbers written on the box, and by the size printed inside the shoe, *not* by whether or not it actually fits! If a lady thinks she wears a 5AAA, it doesn't matter if the shoe is a 4B, as long as the box or the inside of the shoe *says* it's a 5AAA!

Feet surely are different. There are big little toes, and little big toes. There are short toes where there should be long toes, and long toes where God must have intended short ones.

And what is true of feet goes for ears, too. Have you ever noticed people's ears—or looked at yours in the mirror? Maybe one ear is higher than the other, or one is plastered back against the head while the other is waving like a flag, or looks like you've got the flaps down for landing!

And what's true of people's looks is true of people's lives. Nobody is perfect. We are all imperfect in both our looks and our lives. Probably the most common phrase in any language is this: "If I just had it to do over again . . ." How many times have you said that?

"Oh, if I could just do it over again!" We say it about marriages that don't work; report cards that aren't up to par; job interviews that fall through; business deals that don't pan out. What we are really saying is "If I only had a second chance!" We want another chance to be what we could be; to be what we want to be; to do what we can do.

I have also noticed that in some of those occasions when we are most likely to say, "If only I had a second chance!" there is a hardness, a harshness, a brittleness, a sense of finality. When we feel there is no second chance, we often feel unforgiven and burdened with failure.

It is true concerning things and of people. That, by the way, is why my flying career was rather brief. I soon discovered that without an instructor in the cockpit with you, there are some things that must be done right the first time or you won't get an opportunity to try again!

In the area of human relationships this feeling of no second chance—and therefore the feeling of failure, of finality, of brittleness, and unforgivenness—is most sadly demonstrated in the tragedy of divorce. I see people all the time who feel there is no second chance in this area, who feel they are failures, even to God and surely to themselves.

I Hear a Whisper

Yet, in spite of our own sinful tendencies and "the school of hard knocks" which screams at us we are no good, something in us whispers the gospel of the second chance. And that still, small voice doesn't come from the world—it comes from God, our Creator. That divine whisper keeps saying deep down in our souls, "Try again. There is a second chance." Listen carefully—hear that tiny voice?

The Bible is all about this gospel of the second chance. That's what Noah's ark is all about; that's what the rainbow is all about—a second chance. God's intention is that all us Adams and Eves who have lost our Eden have a second chance. That's what the touching story in Genesis about

Abraham trying to talk God out of destroying Sodom and Gomorrah is all about—a second chance for sinners.

That's why we get a lump in our throats when we hear the story of Joseph and how, way down in Egypt, he was raised above his adversity to become the second most powerful man in the world. Remember in that glorious forty-fifth chapter of Genesis how Joseph told his guilty brothers not to worry about the past, but go get Papa and let's start all over here in Egypt—a second chance!

That's what Hosea is preaching in his story of a young husband so deeply in love with an unfaithful wife that he never really gets over her, and in the end welcomes her back into his home and heart—the gospel of the second chance. When you read that short story of the little man and the big fish, you know it's not really about Jonah or Nineveh, but about a gospel of a second chance—for both the prophet and the wicked city. And when you come to the New Testament and read the earliest account of the life and death of Jesus ever written, it is from the pen of John Mark, a man who got a second chance.

That's what Jesus preached—the gospel of the second chance. God is not in the business of putting people down—that's the devil's stock in trade! If I read the book right, God is in the business of giving sinners a second chance through Jesus Christ.

We are all familiar with the stories Jesus told. Of all the perceptive parables He gave us, which is most beloved to Christians of every land and age? It by far the story of the Prodigal Son. And consider it—a powerful way of putting the gospel of the second chance. The boy was lost—now he's found; dead—but now he's alive! Let's welcome the sinner back home!

Jesus demonstrated His gospel of the second chance in His actions. Our text passage is about the adulteress, a woman who was given a second chance. Not because she had earned it, or deserved it, but because she needed a second chance! None of us deserve the second chance, or third, or fourth, or fifth chance that God gives us, but we sorely need it.

What a joy it is to preach the gospel of the second chance, to say to people, "If you will accept it, God believes in you and wants to give you a second chance!" I once preached a series of monologue sermons about a character I named Harold, basing the sermons on my experiences with a transient who desperately needed a second chance. Some months later the man, who had begun to put his life together with God's help, joined our church. We have kept in touch, and only recently he went to work in a business owned by one of our church families. He is doing well and grateful that God and our church felt him worthy of a second chance.

How Jesus Offered the Second Chance in His Last Week

To see how this gospel of the second chance permeated the ministry of Jesus, consider with me the last week of His earthly life. Let us consider the feast at Bethany, in the twelfth chapter of John's Gospel. Jesus and His disciples were there, sitting at a table with Lazarus. Martha, as was her custom, was busy with the domestic chores of such an occasion; but where was Mary? Mary broke the jar containing the pound of ointment of spikenard, anointed the feet of

Jesus, and wiped them with her hair. The whole house was filled with the sweet perfume.

Why did Mary do this? Some folks claim it is because Jesus had given her a second chance somewhere, sometime earlier in His ministry. Possible, but I feel it is more likely she broke the alabaster jar of perfume and anointed the Lord's feet, not necessarily because He gave her a second chance, but rather out of gratitude for the second chance He gave her brother Lazarus in raising him from the dead! Can you imagine what changes were made in Lazarus' life because of this gift!

Later in this final week, we come to the Last Supper—note Luke's account in chapter 22. Jesus makes the beautiful promise to His disciples that they will eat and drink at His table in His kingdom. Then we read a touching exchange between Peter and Christ:

> And the Lord said, Simon, Simon, behold, Satan hath desired to have you, that he may sift you as wheat: But I have prayed for thee, that thy faith fail not: and when thou art converted, strengthen thy brethren. And he said unto him, Lord, I am ready to go with thee, both into prison, and to death. And he said, I tell thee, Peter, the cock shall not crow this day, before that thou shalt thrice deny that thou knowest me (vv. 31-34).

Isn't that beautiful? Christ knew all about how fickle, how boastful Peter was. He already knew Peter was going to deny Him, yet He still loved Peter, was going to pray for him, and would give him another chance. Indeed, one of the glorious facets of the resurrection is the angel's message to go and tell His disciples—and especially Peter!

Go with the tiny band as they finish the Last Supper and

walk down to the Kidron Valley and over to the little garden called Gethsemane. Before long the vigil of prayer is broken by approaching torchlight and the mumble of voices. As this second group reaches the garden there is an embarrassed pause, then Judas steps forward and greets the Master with a kiss.

That hell-tormented man, even now tottering on the brink of eternity without God, would deny his dearest friend with a kiss! But Jesus' response to this act of betrayal was to call him "Friend." Even at that point, Jesus would have given (and was giving) the possibility of a second chance to Judas. But Judas was blind to that possibility, and after remorse set in, he saw no way out but suicide. The main difference between Judas and Peter was that Judas never grasped the gospel of the second chance, whereas Peter did.

But let us go from the garden to Caiaphas's house, and then to the meeting with Pilate. And, marvel of marvels, see this good news of a second chance demonstrated even by a pagan, as Pilate tries to give Jesus a second chance, to no avail.

And so the slow march to Calvary began. The crown of thorns was yanked off so it would not be lost on the way—they would "crown" him again with it when He was fixed on the cross. Soon the Maker of all creation was hanging between heaven and earth, every breath sheer torture. Through eyes blinded with staring at that swirling orb He looked at His tormenters, and through lips parched by the broiling sun He said, "Father, forgive them, for they know not what they do." And that translates into this—"Father, give them a second chance!" And if there's a second chance for even such as they, there is a second chance for you.

Truths of the Gospel of the Second Chance

The gospel of the second chance is for *all,* not merely the slightly soiled. From the tortured soul of the adulteress to the hopeless, helpless thief on the cross—this gospel is for everyone, including the one of whom Charles Wesley wrote:

> Depth of mercy! can there be
> Mercy still reserved for me?
> Can my God His wrath forbear?
> Me, the chief of sinners spare?
>
> I have long withstood His grace;
> Long provoked Him to His face;
> Would not hear His gracious calls;
> Grieved Him by a thousand falls.[1]

How well I remember the story, learned when I was a college student studying German, of the tramp found in the gutters of a German city. This was long ago, in days when European medical students used the unclaimed bodies of the unfortunate as laboratory cadavers. Two students approached the dead body of the tramp, and one of them remarked that this was a worthless one, who had no value either alive or dead. Suddenly the "corpse" answered their comment: "Nennen sie kein mann wertlos für den der Christus hat gestorben!" "Call no man worthless for whom Christ has died!" Every person is precious to God.

Secondly, this gospel of the second chance is *from God.* John 3:16 plainly tells us our second chance for a meaningful life is not the result of our hands, but the result of God's heart. We do not *naturally* give people a second chance, or a third, or a fourth. Perhaps if they are our flesh and blood, or someone we want to impress or manipulate, we will be very forgiving and generous—but our *nature* is to demand perfection the first time around, even though we ourselves are imperfect! And when we do try to live an accepting and forgiving life-style, the motivation is from God in Christ.

Thirdly, this gospel of the second chance is a *costly gift from God.* The parable of the vineyard leaves no doubt that Jesus saw himself as the son of the owner whose life was forfeited. My hometown of Madison, Florida, is a typical Southern county-seat town. In the center of the town is the courthouse, and directly across from it is the Confederate Park. In the park is a lovely monument to a local hero, medal of honor winner Colin P. Kelly, Jr. Four tall angels represent freedom from want, freedom from fear, freedom of speech, and freedom of worship. They remind us that these were bought at a terrible price in the Second World War. At the base of the statue John 15:13 is inscribed: "Greater love hath no man than this, that a man lay down his life for his friends." The statue speaks of a man's sacrifice, but a greater sacrifice by Jesus Christ, God incarnate, is revealed in the verse. Jesus is more than a man, and His death is more than one man dying for another man. It is God suffering for sinful mankind, all sinful people throughout the years of time, and giving them a second chance.

Fourthly, this gospel of the second chance is a *matter of faith.* God has already acted on His faith in man, by sending Jesus to die for our sins. God could have simply wiped the slate clean, flicked this old world into the next cosmos with His finger, and started all over with a new creation. But He didn't, choosing instead to give us a second chance. Now the act of faith is up to each of us, to respond to God's faith in us.

Years ago Georgia Tech and Cal Tech played in the Rose Bowl. Cal Tech player Roy Riegels hauled in a fumble; reversed his field, cut, circled, saw a hole—and scrambled for pay dirt. He wondered, however, as he ran for all he was worth, why his own teammates were screaming at him and still more confused as to why one of them finally tackled him and brought him down—only then did he learn that he had galloped sixty-three yards toward the wrong goal post! You can imagine his feelings at the half when the teams went into the locker room. He wanted to die; he had never been so embarrassed! But the storm never broke; the coach said absolutely nothing about Roy's colossal blunder. Then the whistle sounded for the second half and the coach said, "All right, Roy, the game is only half over—get back into the game!" I'm sure he played like never before in that second half, like Peter, the adulteress, the centurion, and millions more in the twenty centuries since the cross.

Finally, this gospel of the second chance is *a dynamic of love.* I saw an enchanting article in a newspaper not long ago. Very few men have the opportunity of falling in love twice with the same woman. Yet that's what happened to Larry Krusinski. He became an amnesia victim following a traffic accident which left him in a coma for ten days. When he awoke he was paralyzed and could not remember being married for three years. Mrs. Krusinski said she just kept telling him she loved him, visiting him in the hospital, and bringing him his favorite food, pizzas—even though he didn't know who she was. "Finally he started liking me," she said. It seems that Larry has fallen in love all over again with the same woman! His wife Janet said, "I've set aside a few of my dreams for awhile, but it doesn't matter because I love him. Nothing is hard when someone loves you back."

God had to lay aside some divine dreams because first, Adam, and now each of us in turn, have developed a spiritual amnesia called sin. But God has declared lovingly in His Word that in the cross, even though some of His dreams for your life and mine have had to be laid aside for awhile because of our unbelief and sinfulness, it's all right, because He loves us.

"Depth of mercy, can there be/Mercy yet reserved for me?" There can be, and is, if you will accept the gospel of the second chance!

21
The King Is Coming: Closing Time
Matthew 25:31-46

But the day of the Lord will come as a thief in the night (2 Pet. 3:10).

One of the unlikely topics in the 1984 presidential debates between Ronald Reagan and Walter Mondale was Armageddon. Along with many others, I suspected the references to biblical prophecies concerning the end of the world were simple trappings of religious terminology for politics' sake.

Nevertheless, it reminded me of a story which was making the rounds. In the late 1950s when our country was in an extremely science-oriented mood, a group of scientists were meeting to decide mathematically and objectively how this world is going to come to an end. As they sat in their committees theorizing, suddenly the clatter of keys and slamming of a door were heard, and behind them stood God, who said with a smile—"Closing time, Gentlemen!" While we mere humans can never pinpoint the hour, there *is* a closing time decreed for earth in the timetable of God.

Now Jesus' teachings can be arranged around two stackpoles: the Father and the Father's kingdom. We are to be like the Father, and we are to seek the Father's kingdom. But if, in the end of everything, there is no reward, no inheritance for the saints in light, then the concept of the Father is a vain delusion. If, in the end, that kingdom we are told to seek does not materialize, if good does not win out over evil, then the idea of the kingdom is an empty dream.

Jesus proclaimed both the Father and His kingdom, and undergirded His teaching about both by proclaiming that whatever the course of history might be, the end is victory in God! Furthermore, Jesus spoke of this unraveling of the sleeve of time, this cutting of the knot of sin's power, this handing over of the Kingdom to the saints, in the context of *His coming again.*

Jesus Will Come Again

In the parable of the sheep and goats we read that when the Son of man comes in His glory, before Him shall all the nations be gathered. Paul writes that at the sound of the trumpet the Lord shall descend and the dead in Christ shall rise. Timothy is admonished: "I charge thee therefore before God, and the Lord Jesus Christ who shall judge the quick and the dead at his appearing and his kingdom" (2 Tim. 4:1). Even the writer of 2 Peter speaks of the return of Jesus as the sign for the crumbling of this old world order. Again and again Jesus' return is tied to resurrection, judgment, and a new world. Let us, then, look at the biblical teaching as to events which will take place at Jesus' return, and what this will mean to you and me.

However, I warn you at the start that the Bible does not set forth any detailed scheme concerning events of the end. Apparently Jesus was not concerned with our knowing the specific details of the world's "closing time." If it had been important, if it were imperative that we know these things—

then Jesus would have certainly told us. What Jesus emphasized, and what I would be faithful in emphasizing to you, is the importance of our being prepared for the end of this world and the coming of Jesus.

But many well-intentioned folks persist in scheming out the future. Not long ago, I received in the mail an Armageddon calendar. This calendar, emphasized the letter which came with it, could reveal to me the signs of the end time, almost month by month. Some folks say the Jewish Temple must be rebuilt in Jerusalem before Jesus comes back; others teach a "secret" rapture of the church before the end; others preach a tribulation period and/or a millennium reign in connection with Jesus' return. However good many of these detailed outlines look when built on selected proof texts, I feel each has serious problems when the whole counsel of the New Testament is considered.

Years ago while leading revival services in the church where I was pastor, a friend preached a sermon in which he proclaimed that 200 million horses of a special breed were being prepared in Russia. This, he declared, was in direct fulfillment of prophecy concerning the last days. After that service, as we walked away from the darkened church, I asked him, "Tell me, do you *really* believe that stuff you were saying?" His answer was, "Well, honestly, I don't think it will have to happen like that, but folks won't come unless we preach that way!"

I feel that approach is bad for at least two good reasons. First, I think God's people are mature enough to receive the Bible in its unvarnished, plain, clear truth. In the second place, such twisting of the symbolic teaching of the Bible is irresponsible on the part of supposedly mature Bible teachers. I stand squarely in the midst of evangelical scholarship when I declare there is no detailed scheme of the last times in the Bible.

The Bible does give us *broad outlines* of the end. In the broad strokes of "brushes of comets' hair" and on a "ten league canvas," the biblical artists painted the drama of the last times.

We will not go far wrong if we base our ideas of the end time on the what the Bible says about the following themes: the literal return of Jesus, at whose appearing the resurrection of the dead and the transformation of the living Christians will take place; then comes the great judgment, the partition of souls, the dissolution of this present world order, and heaven and hell.

What Happens to Me After Death?

The doctrine of *the resurrection of the dead* may speak to you in the question, "What happens to me when I die?" There are four major views concerning life after death. First is the idea that *death means the end of everything*—body and soul. Most folks who reject God feel that when you die, that's all. This is *not* biblical.

A second view is that when we die we *receive an interim body* for the interval between our death and the second coming of Jesus. I cannot find a basis for this in the New Testament. A third view was taught by Martin Luther and others; the idea of "soul sleep"—that is, from our death until the "great gittin' up mornin' " *we simply sleep in the grave.* This view is the result of misunderstanding symbolic language.

I believe the Bible teaches another view, that *the Chris-*

tian is very much alive during the time between his death and Jesus' return—but that we simply have no body! This is made clear by Paul in his letters (see Phil. 1:23-24; 2 Corinthians 5:1-10; 1 Thess. 4:13-18). Paul indicates, as does Jesus, that the Christian goes immediately to be with God. Paul speaks of yearning to go and be with God, yet he expresses fear in 2 Corinthians 5:1-2 of being "unclothed," or being without a physical body. He desired rather to remain until Jesus' return and be "clothed upon," that is, given his new spiritual body without tasting of death. He goes on to elaborate his teaching that at the return of Jesus, the Christian will receive a resurrection body. Those Christians still living on that day will be "clothed upon" with their new bodies.

One more word about our resurrection bodies. Some folks feel this new body will bear the marks and scars of our earthly pilgrimage, as Jesus' body bore the nailprints during his postresurrection appearances. To insist that we bear even into eternity the marks of our earthly pilgrimage is not to speak of true *resurrection* for the Christian, but *resuscitation* of the old body! The Bible does not tell us our bodies will be like Jesus' body was immediately after His resurrection, with its marks of His sufferings for His disciples, and especially Thomas, to ponder. There was an obvious reason for this kind of appearance; it was an aid to faith. Not even in 1 Corinthians, as Paul searches for a good illustration of our glorious resurrection bodies, does he use Jesus' body as a model. The Bible teaches *resurrection,* a body free from decay and death, a body fitted for heaven—not a resuscitation of *this* body, old, broken, and disfigured.

That Great Judgment Day

When Jesus comes back, not only will there be a resurrection of the dead and a transformation of the living, but there will also be a *final judgment.* Now, our minds are filled with a lot of housekeeping questions about the final judgment. I keep hearing folks ask such questions as: "How long will it take to judge everybody who has ever lived?" "If we go immediately to heaven or hell upon death, why call us back to a judgment?" "Will actual books be opened, and how many pages will my book have?"

Such questions are understandable, but they really show the finiteness of our minds, and our inability to grasp the fullness of eternal truth about the final judgment. I heard a missionary say recently that if a person were baptized each minute, we would not have baptized a billion people in these 2000 years of the Christian era! So, obviously, God cannot judge each person in a literal courtroom scene.

Some folks teach multiple judgments. In the mid-nineteenth century an English preacher named Darby constructed an end-time scheme in which he divided the history of the world into redemptive dispensations, with three judgments at the end. Rev. C.I. Scofield then popularized this view in his *Scofield Bible,* aided by the failure of many people to distinquish between Scofield's notes and the Scripture text!

This threefold judgment (which I do not endorse) features first the sheep and goats judgment, a judging of nations during the tribulation, a seven-year period of time. While the tribulation runs its course on earth, the secretly raptured church is judged in heaven at the judgment seat of Christ. The third judgment is that which takes place in the air at the end of time, while the world burns below, a judgment of all the ages and is called the great white throne judgment. Now all this is extremely picturesque, but I feel it is not very biblical.

The clearest teaching of the Bible on the topic seems to be *one judgment, which will include everyone.* That will be a great day of *revealing and unveiling.* We can get the idea by thinking of the tearing down of an old building. There is a sense of awe, even reverence, as huge foundation sills are exposed to daylight again; as the sunlight strikes dust hidden in darkness for perhaps a century. And if you look closely, you may find the initials of the carpenter, carved on a heavy beam and hidden away these many years.

In just such an awesome and revealing way our lives will open up to the scrutiny of the sunlight of God. What will be unveiled? Our sins, obviously. Everyone expects *that* calamity as a matter of course! In recent days there seems to be a tremendous concern in our city—at least on the part of the police—in keeping folks within the speed limit. All of which is to say that within a three-week period three members of my church staff and my daughter received traffic tickets. I suppose it's really not a big deal, but nobody likes to be pulled over on a main street, and have all your friends come by while the policeman is writing out your traffic ticket, his blue lights flashing! Now traffic tickets have to be paid. And our sins must be paid for as well. If you and I sinned only once a day—an impossibility in itself—we would rack up over 25,000 sins in seventy years. And we are just speaking of overt, outward actions of disobedience and rebellion toward God. To show the seriousness of our sins, let's assume every sin is a traffic ticket. Could you stand before a judge and look him in the eye and tell him you're sorry about those 25,000 tickets and expect him to let it go at that?

Yet I would stress that while your sins may be hideous, they are *not* the most terrible aspect of your life which will be revealed, nor will the evil deeds you have done send you to hell! The judgment will reveal a more drastic matter: *our saving relationship—or lack of it—to Jesus Christ.* It is your lack of a saving relationship to Jesus that will consign you to hell. That day will reveal the sentence each of us has passed on himself as we decided what to do with Jesus during the days of our lives.

Look with me briefly at one other aspect of the end—the destruction of the present world order. Like many of you, I can easily see the possibility of our blowing this entire globe into eternity in an nuclear war. And, while 2 Peter 3 may, in the minds of many, be an apt description of such an end—I seriously doubt that God was concerned with such a description when He inspired Peter to write to beleaguered Christians of the first century.

The Bible says the heavens and earth will be removed, and there will be a *new* heavens and earth, a new creation, full of righteousness. Some folks think heaven itself will be this renewed earth. I don't know, and the Bible is certainly not clear. I'll trust Jesus—He said He was going to prepare *a place* for His people.

When The King Comes Again

But what is all this teaching about the end point to? All this biblical symbolism leading up to? What does it mean to you and me? Two paradoxes sum up what I have been saying in this message.

First, I believe *the coming of the King is going to mean separation and reunion.* Remember the parable of the tares? Let both weed and seed grow until the day of harvest, and *then* they will be separated. In the parable of the net the fishermen scoop up all kinds of fish. "But in the last days," says Jesus, "the angels will sort them out." Separation! Indeed, *the ultimate meaning of hell is separation from God.* This modern heresy that everything is going to turn out all right in the end is sheer folly and leads to destruction! When the King comes it will be a time of separation.

Paradoxically, the end will be a *time of reunion.* For those who love God it will be a time of reunion with those whom we have loved and lost for awhile. If it is not so that heaven means reunion with Jesus and our friends, then all Jesus said at that supper table to the disciples was vain and empty talk; the keeping of a stiff upper lip in the face of oblivion. But I am persuaded that Jesus has gone to prepare a place for us.

One other paradox: *When the King comes it will be both the end and the beginning.* It will be the end of many things, for, after all, when we speak of the end of the world, in our finite minds we are simply planting a signpost at the limits of our spiritual perception. It will be the end of man's struggle with his sinful nature; the end of the Christian's struggle with corruption and death. "Death, where is thy sting? O grave, where is thy victory?" (1 Cor. 15:55). It will be the end of overleaping ambition and greed which rules in men's hearts now. It will be the end of God's lonely, heartbreaking search for the lost child. It will be the end of sermons, of invitations to take Christ as Savior, of pleadings with the lost sinner.

They said, time and time again, that it was the end, the defeat of God. They said it was the end when Herod took his sword and bathed it in blood at Bethlehem when the King was born. They said it was the end when Pilate washed his hands in the basin declaring, "His blood be on [*you*]." They said it was the end when the soldiers' hammer blows echoed across the Hill of the Skull. They said it was the end when the priests walked by, sneering and saying, "If he be [God], let him come down." They said it was the end when he cried out, "My God, my God, why hast thou forsaken me?" They said it was the end when he laid his fevered head back on the rough cross and died. They said it was the end when Pilate put a guard at his grave and dared him to come out. They said it was the end when the crowd laughed and jeered at the eleven and said, "[They] are full of new wine" (Acts 2:13). They said it was the end when a brilliant young Pharisee named Paul went forth to conquer the church. They said it was the end when Simon Peter, obeying God rather than men, sat down at the table with Gentiles. They said it was the end when Paul was stoned at Lystra and left for dead. They said it was the end when Peter was crucified upside down and Paul was beheaded.

But it *wasn't* the end, and it *won't* be the end, until the sun stops shining and the world stops turning, and the King comes swinging the eternal keys, saying, "Closing time, boys," and the "great gittin' up mornin'" has come and Jesus begins to reign over every heart!

Then it will be the *end,* and paradoxically, it will also be the *beginning.* For, after all, it will just be the beginning for God's people: "Eye hath not seen, nor ear heard, nor have entered into the heart of man, the things which God hath prepared for them who love him" (1 Cor. 2:9).

> "When we've been there ten thousand years,
> Bright shining as the sun,
> We've no less days to sing God's grace,
> Than when we'd first begun."
>
> —John Newton

Have you made your preparations for the end? What if it should be today?

Notes

Chapter 1

1. James Weldon Johnson, *God's Trombones* (New York: Viking Press, 1927), pp. 21-26.
2. Ian Maclaren, *Beside the Bonnie Brier Bush* (Chicago: M. A. Donahue & Co., n. d.), pp. 110-138.

Chapter 3

1. George Bernanos, *The Diary of a Country Priest,* quoted in Paul Scherer, *The Word God Sent* (Grand Rapids: Baker Book House, 1965), p. 60.

Chapter 4

1. Clovis Chappell, *Chappell's Special Day Sermons* (Grand Rapids: Baker Book House, 1964), pp. 63-64.

Chapter 5

1. By his friends, *G. A. Studdert-Kennedy* (London: Hodder & Stoughton, 1929), p. 133.
2. Dale Moody, *The Word of Truth* (Grand Rapids: William B. Eerdmans Publishing Company, 1981), pp. 309-311.
3. William Barclay, *The Revelation of John,* Vol. 2 (Edinburgh: The Saint Andrew Press, 1959), p. 254.

Chapter 6

1. See Albert Schweitzer, *The Quest of the Historical Jesus.* trans. J. R. Coates (London: A. and C. Black, Ltd., 1954), especially pp. 349-401.
2. See Hans Küng, *On Being a Christian,* trans. Edward Quinn (Garden City, NY: Doubleday and Company, 1976), especially pp. 119-165.

3. Drama by Lenore Coffee and William Joyce Corven, quoted in Paul E. Scherer, *For We Have This Treasure* (Grand Rapids: Baker Book House, 1944), pp. 101.

Chapter 7

1. Helen Keller, "Three Days to See," originally published in The *Atlantic Monthly,* condensed in *The Reader's Digest Reader,* Theodore Roosevelt, editor (Garden City, NY: Garden City Publishing, Company, Inc., n. d.), pp. 213-215.

Chapter 8

1. Paul Tournier, *The Person Reborn,* trans. Edwin Hudson (New York: Harper & Row, 1966), pp. 230-231.

Chapter 11

1. Anna Talbott McPherson, *They Dared to Be Different* (Chicago: Moody Press, 1967), p. 146.

Chapter 12

1. Sally Magnusson, *The Flying Scotsman* (New York: Quartet Books, 1981), p. 37.
2. Quoted in H. Wheeler Robinson, *The Christian Experience of the Holy Spirit* (London: Fontana Books, 1962), p. 78.
3. Paul Scherer, *For We Have This Treasure* (Grand Rapids: Baker Book House, 1976), p. 80.
4. "Ready," words by A. C. Palmer.
5. Quoted in Magnusson, p. 165.
6. Ibid., p. 169.

Chapter 13

1. Article in the *Memphis Commercial Appeal,* Memphis, Tennessee, June 25, 1984.

Chapter 14

1. Powhatan W. James, *George W. Truett: A Biography* (New York: The Macmillan Company, 1945), pp. 85-89.

Chapter 18

1. For this bit of poetry and some of the seed ideas of this sermon, I am indebted to my college pastor, colleague, and friend, Dr. J. Winston Pearce. His sermon, "Heaven's Gates and the Gypsies," may be found in his book, *The Window Sill of Heaven* (Broadman Press: Nashville, 1958), pp. 123-131.

2. Ernest W. Bacon, *Spurgeon: Heir of the Puritans* (Grand Rapids: William B. Eerdmans Publishing Company, 1967), p. 170.